PRAISE FROM A

MW00944886

FINDING PEACE - WHEN THE DEVIL VISITS

"A story that will break your heart over and over again...and then amaze you about the strength of the human spirit. It is possible to break the chains of family dysfunction!"

—**K. Truly Campbell**, LAPC

(Licensed Associate Professional Counselor)

"Is it possible that a victim's greatest triumph comes upon the road of forgiveness? Mechelle McDermott's compelling book suggests so. Sharing her own personal story as a victim of abuse and abandonment, Mechelle shows that a victim's ultimate victory comes from courageously rising above a tragic past and then creating a personal future full of brightness and hope. One cannot do it alone. It requires taking the hand of God, and Mechelle is living proof that some of God's finest children have risen out of some of the devil's darkest playgrounds."

—**Blenda McGary,** Inspirational Pianist/ Composer, *Blenda McGary Music*

"Having seen similar heart-break in the medical field, healthcare workers such as myself should reflect on how often we may have failed to recognize the devastating effect suicide has on surviving relatives and friends and the compassion and support we can provide to them. This story reveals how the human spirit can shine and not be ruined in the darkest of hours and personal catastrophes. Mechelle's book reminds us that with faith and love we can be strong enough to let go and close some of life's most difficult doors, find hope, happiness and become the change we wish to see in our life and the world."

—**Linda Robertson**, Registered Nurse/Risk Manager

"From the first page to the last, When the Devil Visits is a gripping story of faith and forgiveness. Even with the most tragic of events, the author presses on to eventually overcome the perils and brokenness of childhood abandonment including the death of those most loved. She shines light in the darkest of darkness, encouraging the reader to press on…there is hope."

—**Vicki Hewitt**, CEO Custom Imprint America

Mechelle R. McDermott

Finding Peace
WHEN
THE DEVIL
VISITS

FindingPeace When the Devil Visits
Copyright © 2015 by Mechelle R. McDermott. All rights reserved.

CI Marketing, cimprint@msn.com

Published in the United States of America

ISBN-13: 978-1508670834
ISBN-10: 1508670838
BISAC: Biography & Autobiography / Personal Memoirs

Jerry and Claudette Martin
Married September 11, 1959

Acknowledgments

I would like to thank my cousin Sheri for being a kindred spirit and helping me through just about every year of my life. You are truly an amazing person of insight and love, and I believe you were placed in my life to get me through the hardest parts.

I'm grateful to each of my children: Katryna, Lucas, Danielle, Brittany, Hannah, Mikayla, and Cody. You are the breath of my existence. You too have been placed in my life to help me grow a new heart after the first one was shattered. You have spiritual gifts and talents I can only dream of having.

I can never adequately thank my husband, Reed, for living through my struggles with me again and again, and comforting me through the losses. You are truly my other half.

DEDICATION

To my posterity, may this book be a beacon light to generations yet unborn.

Sometimes you find yourself in the middle of nowhere, and sometimes in the middle of nowhere, you find yourself.

—Unknown

CONTENTS

THE DEVIL LEAVES HIS CALLING CARD

APRIL 23, 1978
GILA BEND, ARIZONA

What is the police car doing in my driveway? I thought to myself as I was coming up the street to go home after school. I was barely sixteen and afraid I had done something wrong.

I was baffled, curious, and worried, all at once. I knew Dad wasn't home; he had left for a business trip to Wyoming. I hadn't seen my mom for a few days because she said she was visiting friends, but maybe she came home while I was at school.

I slowly pulled into the driveway next to the officer. I got out of the car, walked over to his window, and asked sheepishly, "Can I help you?"

"Do you know where your father is?" he asked. He had a very serious tone in his voice. He was young with dark hair, and his face had a serious look to it.

"He's out of town, but he is supposed to be coming back today." I wasn't sure, but that was the last bit of information I had.

He seemed a little agitated by my answer and looked like he really needed to contact my father. I asked if everything was okay. He pushed again. "When do you think he will be home?"

"I thought he was coming back from Wyoming, and I don't know when he will be home. Do you want to talk to my mother?" I said in a pleasing voice.

That was when he relented and started to divulge more information.

"Your mother is in the hospital in Litchfield. She is in a coma from trying to commit suicide," he said without emotion.

My heart sank. It was surreal to hear him say that. Thinking he might drive off before I would know, I quietly asked one more question, "What happened?"

"I don't know much except that she took an overdose of pills at the Cosmo's Bar about ten miles outside of town, and someone called an ambulance. If you see your father, tell him to call the police department," he said while writing a few more notes on his notepad.

He proceeded to pull out of the driveway and drove away. I wasn't sure what to do next. I only had my driver's license for a few months, and I had not driven in traffic in the larger suburbs of Phoenix. I vaguely remembered where Litchfield was. It was about forty minutes away. I only knew the name of the town because my mother had a friend she would visit there. *What should I do? Do I try to find the hospital? How do I find my dad?* I tried to be brave, but I just started crying instead.

I ran into the house for the phone book, and there was a small map in the back. The hospital was about forty-five minutes away. I did remember how to get to Interstate 10, on the other side of Buckeye; I just needed to know which exit to take.

I reached the hospital and asked for Claudette Martin's room. Upon entering, I was surprised to see my dad was sitting there! His eyes were red and swollen from crying. He looked tired. He was wearing his usual mechanic work clothes: a denim shirt with denim jeans with a few faded grease spots on his jeans and a pack of cigarettes tucked in the pocket with a western-cut pocket flap snapped shut. His face had years of exposure from the Arizona sun, and it had faded shades of deep red along the neckline. His hair was oily from his VO5 hair cream and slightly uncombed.

I could smell the plastic from the tubes and cleaners in the room. My mom was hooked up to tubes and wires, and she was sleeping. I could hear the evenly spaced *beep, beep, beep* on the machine recording her heart rate.

I hugged Dad and asked him what happened and how did he find out.

"I was pulled over by a policeman an hour outside of Flagstaff because there was an APB [all-points bulletin] on my truck, and I was told to go to the hospital," he said.

He proceeded to tell me that when he walked in, she started to wake up and, as she was ripping the wires off her, was screaming, "Let me die! Let me die!" The nurse ran in and sedated her, and she was sleeping now.

He struggled to tell me the rest of the story, knowing I was looking for more answers.

He began, "I had confronted your mom last night on the phone about her affair with another man named Carson Booker. Carson had met her at her salon and was spending too much time with her daily at the salon. I asked her to choose between the two of us. She said she couldn't choose between the two of us." His voice started to crack as his eyes began to tear up.

He continued, "This morning, she began drinking and taking prescription pills until she passed out at Cosmos Bar located about ten miles out of town. The bar owner called an ambulance for her. The paramedics arrived and performed CPR on her, and brought her to the hospital. Her chest had bruises where they tried to save her."

He started to cry, and now the tears rolled down his cheeks. He wiped the tears, and he recounted how much he loved her and wanted to work things out with her.

"That was why I went to Wyoming. I wanted to sell my diesel mechanic shop in Gila Bend and move the family away so she could not be near Carson anymore," he said.

The room was silent except for the beeping noise on the heart monitor. He said very little, and he was done talking. Dad was not a man of words. He was usually quiet, and this was the first time in my life I had heard him express any feelings or cry. He stood up and said he needed to go for something to eat and drink, and that he would be back in about an hour. I didn't ask to go along; I sensed he wanted his privacy so he could gather his thoughts and feelings.

"I'll be right here, Dad," I said, trying to assure him he was not alone.

I sat there staring at my mother. I just kept feeling Dad's sorrow, feeling shocked that my mother had tried to kill herself, and I was feeling helpless that I couldn't help either one of them.

My mind was running wild with so many questions: Why was Mom doing this? Was Carson really ten years younger than her? What could Carson give her that my father didn't? Why did he think it was okay to start an affair with a married woman who had five children? Who was this guy? How come I have never heard of him in this small town? Was this why my mom was leaving for days at a time?

I just stared at the equipment and followed the wires and hoses leading to each part of my mother's body. I couldn't believe this was happening. My thoughts took me back to my childhood.

My parents married young at the ages of fifteen and eighteen in 1959. They are thirty-three and thirty-six respectively now. They had struggled to provide for five children. Dad had always worked two jobs and looked tired. Mom was a full-time homemaker, except for when she went to beauty school. She had just opened her own salon a few months ago. She felt her children were old enough not to require a babysitter anymore, and our small town did not have a place to get your hair cut.

They had their disagreements over the years, but this was new. I had never seen something this serious threatening our family. My mind reviewed what little I had known. Over the years, Mom and Dad had fights and arguments, but always made up.

A few days before Dad left for Wyoming, he and Mom were fighting, and I asked him to sit in my car with me so we could talk. He wasn't willing to share with me what they were fighting about, so I just started telling him how important he was to our family and how grateful we were to have him provide for us. I went to reach over and hug him, and my hand hit the top of his handgun tucked under his belt.

"Don't try to take it away from me," he said.

"I'm not! What is it?" I said, pretending not to know what it was as I quickly pulled back into my seat. I was scared. I didn't expect him to have a gun, and I didn't know why he had it.

"It's my gun. I just need it with me right now," he said as he was getting out of the car and walking toward the house. He was done talking. Dad usually carried a gun in his truck because of the late-night service calls he would get from stranded truckers.

For as long as I could remember, Dad had worked long hours, usually as a heavy-equipment operator at the copper mines and now as a diesel mechanic. We moved almost every year of my life and sometimes attended two schools in a year as different jobs came open within the network of mines. When the Duval Sierrita mine closed in Tucson, he was asked to stay to help get the heavy-equipment vehicles maintained and ready for sale. This gave him the additional training he need to open his own diesel mechanic shop back in Gila Bend, Arizona, the town he grew up in.

We moved to Gila Bend in 1975. Gila Bend is a small desert town with a mix of farming and a small air force base gunnery range on the outskirts. It is about sixty miles southwest of Phoenix. It is famous for its extreme heat records tying with Death Valley. The town has a sign that says "Gila Bend Welcomes You, Home of 1,700 Friendly People and 5 Old Crabs, Elev. 737 ft." Gila Bend is the gateway from Phoenix to San Diego, California.

Dad ruled with an iron fist, but he was never abusive toward my mother. He was ready to use the belt on any of his children, especially at the request of my mother. My father's parents were farmers, and they raised their children to do hard labor and have the strictest of obedience to their parents. My father tried to emulate that, but we were more afraid of our father than we were respectful of his methods.

Mom was anxious to take Dad out nearly every weekend going to the bars for drinks with friends and dancing. She was always planning a get-together with another couple to come over and play cards. Mom and Dad laughed a lot when around others. She liked to socialize, and I think she liked the attention from the other men as she had a pretty face and would wear fancy head scarves with different wigs and outfits made of polyester, rhinestones, large lapels and bell-bottoms similar to something Elvis Presley wore.

She had the self-perception that her life was as glamorous as any person in Hollywood when she had friends over or when we visited relatives. The real truth was we were a lower-middle-class family, we lived in a single wide trailer with five kids, and neither Mom or Dad had a high school diploma.

The nurse came in and said it would be several hours before she would be awake and that I should go find something to do. I was gripped with fear. I didn't want her to wake up and not have anyone here, but I didn't want to be disobedient either, so I left the room.

I walked slowly down the hallway trying to figure out what the strange smells were about. It was a mix of cleaners and urine probably. I could glance into any rooms that had the doors open and my mind would wonder what each person was in the hospital for.

I stopped for a minute at a bulletin board and read some of the papers pinned to it. It was an incredibly lonely moment. I did not know what to do. I did not even know what to think.

I went outside to sit in my car but decided to go for a drive instead. I had a '68 blue Firebird, with a racing engine in it that my dad and brother restored. The car was initially for my brother but handed down to me. There was a problem that needed fixed, but Dad had not got around to it yet.

I had to crawl under the front side of the driver's side behind the wheel and tap the solenoid with a screwdriver to get the car to start. I was fast at it and looked around to make sure no one could see me to avoid embarrassment. Once it turned on, I jumped up and brushed myself off and put the extra long screwdriver on the floor of the back seat. I sat there in my car for a moment. Confused, hurt, and even frightened. My mom was not making any sense to me.

I didn't know where to go in Litchfield; I was unfamiliar with the surroundings and I didn't have any change with me to even go buy something to drink. It was a warm spring day, so I decided to pull back in the parking lot and wait in my car with the window down for what I thought was an hour and then headed back to look for my dad.

I walked back into the hospital room, and things were not going well at all. Dad was upset, and Mom was missing. To our shock, while we were gone, Carson had been secretly waiting for us to leave the room. Carson told the front desk he was her brother. He entered the room, woke my mother up, and he carried her out of the hospital. The nurse yelled for him to stop but could not get security there in time. The two of them escaped from the hospital together. My father was devastated.

Dad stormed out of the hospital, trying to hold back tears. I told him I would meet him back at the house. Tears were rolling down my cheeks for the forty-minute drive home; I felt my father's pain. I was in over my head. I didn't know how to comfort my dad.

I arrived at home, and the house was empty. *Where is Dad?* I thought I would find my brothers and tell them about what happened and they could help me look for Dad. Then I realized, I didn't even know where to begin looking for Jerry and Scott. They were both in high school, but school had been out for hours now. I called a few phone numbers to see if Dad was at work or if Jerry was at Tess' house, but there were no answers.

I was worried about my two younger siblings, Kristen and Terry, because Mom sent them off to school before she ended up in the hospital. *Where are they?*

Later, I found out the elementary school got news of my mom from the local police department, and the school called a temporary foster home for my two youngest siblings, Kristen and Terry, who were nine and ten at the time.

In my grief and need for more answers, I went to my grandmother's house down the street. She was my mother's mother, and maybe she knew what was going on.

"Grandma, did you know Mom was in the hospital for trying to commit suicide?" I asked.

"Oh no, I did not. What is going on?" she asked as she placed her hand over her mouth in shock.

"Grandma, she tried to take an overdose of pills with alcohol at a bar," I said; then I switched the subject quickly. "What do you know about Carson Booker?"
I could see the surprised look on her face that I knew that name. Grandma just melted. She broke down crying and started spilling the details.

"Your mom has been having an affair with Carson. He has been meeting her at your mother's salon, and your mom was smitten by his compliments and excitement for doing crazy things. She was torn between your dad and her new boyfriend. Carson was living in Yuma, which was about two hours away, and that's why your mom had been gone for days at a time," she said. I could see the frustration starting to kick in because

Grandma was caught. She knew all this and did nothing to stop it.

"What have I done? I don't know what to do. What should I do?" she asked as fear was starting to engulf her.

I barely spoke a word. I was disappointed in my grandmother for keeping it a secret and not trying to stop my mother.

While talking to my grandmother, the phone rang. She argued a little with whoever was on the other end and then apologized. It was my dad.

She looked at me and said, "If you have any way with your father, you should go find him now. He sounds so upset, and I don't think he should be alone right now."

I left her house, drove over to my house, and didn't see his truck. I turned onto the main street and spotted his truck at the Circle K convenience store.

I pulled in just as he was walking out. His eyes were even more red and swollen than when I saw him earlier. He had a bottle wrapped in a brown bag in his hand. I went to hug him, but he pushed me away.

"Leave me alone. I just want to go on a drunk for a few days," he said.

Just then, I glanced in the truck window. On the seat was a pillow, a gray hose, and a roll of tape. I didn't think much of it because he was a mechanic by trade. Maybe he was going to go get drunk and sleep it off.

He stopped for a minute and pulled a wad of rolled-up bills about two thousand dollars in cash out of his shirt pocket.

"Give this to your mom and tell her I said to take care of you kids," he said.

I was a little confused. I was reluctant to try and hug him again after he pushed me away the first time. I said, "Okay," and let him go. He got in his truck and drove away.

Now what? My mom was gone, my dad was upset and leaving for a few days again, my grandmother wouldn't give me the phone number to my mom, and I couldn't find any of my siblings.

Neither Mom nor Dad came home that night, and none of the kids were at the house. I had school the next day, I was emotionally drained, and I decided to go to bed. It was the first time I realized how submissive I was and did not like confrontation. I was concerned about what was going on, and I was too scared to stop my dad, too scared to demand that Grandma give me the phone number where my mom was, or call a friend or neighbor for help.

The next day I went to school. I was on the softball team, and we had a game at Baboquivari after school. The bus rides are usually over an hour to another school because our town is so isolated. This one was over two hours. I can usually get some sleep on the bus, but I was feeling agitated. A strange feeling came over me. I was having flashes in my mind about my dad's truck being in the desert with no roads around it and images of his face with a slight grin. I couldn't figure out why I was having these mental flashes.

I was feeling light-headed and more tired than usual. I just figured I was lacking sleep and emotionally drained from the events at home. However, the images were like lightning bolts that quickly popped into my mind and then would leave. It happened at least three times during the softball game. I ignored those promptings again as there was nothing I could do about them.

The next day was prom, and neither Mom nor Dad was home yet. I was going with my boyfriend, Greg, but I was less than excited because there was no one at the house to share it with, to take pictures with, and to show my dress to. I felt empty inside and wondered if I should even go. The mental flashes came to me again the next day, but what could I do? *What am I supposed to do with those images?*

I got ready for the prom in an empty house. I was so proud of my white Gunne Sax with light-blue ribbons sewn along the edges to give the dress an outline. I was torn between feelings. I wanted to feel pretty, but I knew in my heart something was seriously wrong with my family, and to make matters worse, I had no way to find answers.

Before going to the prom, Greg took me to his house for his mom to take our pictures. He was trying to be funny and light-hearted because he could tell I was withdrawn. We drove to the school and went into the decorated gym. I worried about Greg having a good time because he was four years older than me. I didn't want him to feel out of place. He told me it was no big deal. He knew just about everyone at the school, and it didn't bother him.

I ran into Jerry, but he and Tess were being crowned royalty and having their pictures taken, so I didn't want to drag on their excitement by bringing up Mom and Dad. Later in crossing, I asked him where he had been, and he did tell me that he was staying at Gene's house. He told me not to worry about him, but he had not talked to either Dad or Mom for a few days.

Jerry stayed with his senior-class friends at one table, and Greg and I were on the other side of the gym with my junior-class friends. We danced a few dances, and I wanted to leave. I couldn't get into the prom.

I asked Greg to take me to my grandmother's house. It just felt creepy to be alone in my empty house. He sensed my sadness, and we decided to call it an early night. He dropped me off and said he would see me in the morning at church.

The next morning, my grandmother got up and went to church without me. I told her I was feeling really sad but didn't know why. She told me to go back to sleep and maybe I would feel better later.

About an hour later, I heard someone pulling onto the dirt-and-gravel driveway. I looked out the door, and it was a church member, Wayne Colvin, who was also with the chief of police, John Wike. At that moment, I knew why they were there. A calm voice came to my mind and said, *They are here to tell you about your father.*

Tears started to swell up in my eyes as I opened the door and invited them in. Mr. Colvin said, "Your grandma said we would find you here. We're here to tell you about your father. They found his body this morning."

He started to go into details.

"Your father took a hose, hooked it up to the exhaust, put it through the wing on the driver's side window, and taped it off. He left the truck running and lay down to sleep on the front seat with a pillow. The truck eventually stopped running when it ran out of gas. This allowed the carbon monoxide to come into the cab and cause your dad to go to sleep. It was a painless way to die," he said as his voice trailed off into a somber tone.

I didn't want to hear what he was saying because I wanted to find that place inside of me that was safe. I was terrified. I felt terribly alone at that moment. I started to cry but immediately changed to my brave face. I wanted to cry but not in front of them, and I had this sense of caring for my siblings knowing my mother was missing; I should go find them. All I wanted to do was to go comfort them.

"Thank you for coming. I promise to ask if I need any help," I said. As soon as I closed the door, my tears fell down my face. I just wanted to undo everything I just heard. I put on my shoes while waiting for them to drive off. I then jumped in my car and went to find my siblings.

This time the house wasn't empty as two of my brothers were inside. I ran into the front door, and Jerry and Scott were sitting on the couch next to the door.

"Hey, have you heard?" I asked Jerry.

"Yes, how did you know?" Jerry asked.

"Wayne Colvin and the chief of police found me at Grandma's house after Grandma told them I was there." I said as I reached over to hug Scott. He looked at me to see if I was okay, and I could tell he was trying to be tough and stoic like Jerry. Jerry and Scott both had red eyes. I could tell they had been crying.

Jerry continued to fill me in, "Mom said she will be here today to make funeral arrangements. She said she has Kristen and Terry with her. She wants us three kids to find a place to live."

Jerry was graduating from high school in three weeks. He and Tess had also been making arrangements to get married when they graduated.

Scott, who was only fourteen, said that he would stay with different friends until he could find a permanent place. Scott never did return to school. (This would be the start of his drifter experiences living with different friends, acquaintances, strangers, and occasionally back with Mom over the next few years.)

I asked Grandma if I could stay with her until I found a more permanent place. I wanted to finish out the last few weeks of my junior year of high school at the same school if possible. The only problem with that was Grandma was in no position to take care of anyone. I knew I couldn't stay with Grandma very long because she lived in a one-room shanty that was made from large pieces of tin and wood. Her bed and her couch were in the same room as her kitchen. The shanty didn't have air-conditioning, and in the sweltering summer heat of Arizona, it would often reach up to 110 degrees in the summer.

Grandma wasn't on social security assistance yet; she had one more year. She couldn't feed me or afford to have me stay with her. She was on church assistance for rent and food. She had a couch that I could sleep on. She kept making comments that she loved me, but she didn't know how she was going to take care of me.

I made plans to move in after the funeral. Until then, I would stay at my house.

I just wanted some reassurance from Mom that everything was going to be fine and we were going to be together as a family again, but that never happened. I was miserable. I just wanted to be comforted. I kept crying, and I lost my appetite. I couldn't go to school for a few days because I couldn't stop crying. There was no one at home, and Mom was still not staying at the house. She was staying at Carson's parents' home, a few blocks away.

This was hard for me because over my childhood, I had attached myself to my mother more than to my dad. Although she was manipulative, she wasn't frightening and violent, at times, like Dad. Now she had no need or concern for me. I didn't understand. When I needed her most, she simply was not there for me.

When people would call, Mom was quick to get them off the phone. She wasn't emotional at all and was in a hurry to get the funeral out of the way. She wasn't mourning like the rest of us. She didn't want to be there.

The funeral finally came. The funeral was a strange experience. The chapel had no pews, just folding chairs, and when the people stood up as the family came in, there was the distracting noise of chairs moving. The foyer was full. The chapel had over a hundred people there, many standing along the walls. I didn't recognize anyone. I scanned the room looking for my friends or Greg, and I couldn't find any of them. The funeral was a community spectacle. Many people came to pay respects to my father, but many people who did not know our family came to see the tragic funeral of a suicide victim, who was only thirty-six years old and left five young children behind. This was a big story for such a small town.

This was the first time in my life I had ever been to a funeral. I didn't know what was supposed to happen. We sat on the front row as a family, but I never felt so alone in my life. The casket was about four feet in front of us, and I knew there was no body inside. It was a plastic bag with some of his remains. When a cowboy found his body, he had been in the truck for three days, and in the Arizona heat, his body started to bloat, and when the police tried to move his body out, the body exploded. The police removed some of the body and put it in a plastic bag for the family.

I just stared at the casket and wished I knew exactly who I should direct my thoughts to, my dad or to God. I imagined my dad listening to me as I told him I loved him and was not angry with him. I zoned out the rest of the room. The speaker was talking about the afterlife. I wasn't interested. I just wanted to talk to my dad, and I wasn't even sure he could hear me. My eyes would swell up, and a tear or two would escape, but I was looking for something more. I had spent the last week crying. I was hoping my dad's spirit would be there to comfort me, or someone would say something that would help me to hang on. Nothing—there was nothing to cling to, and at the end of the day, there wasn't anyone around to share my grief with either. My grandma volunteered to stay at home and watch my younger siblings. My mom thought they were too young to attend a funeral.

My father's side of the family was angry with my mother, so there was a divisive feeling in the atmosphere. My aunts, uncles, and grandmother from my father's side did not speak to us children or my mother, and they sat in the back of the chapel.

The music was good. It allowed me to feel something instead of just sadness. I can't remember what the songs were; I just remember stopping my thoughts to feel them. I was glad when the service was over. It seemed boring, and there was no eulogy, so I didn't get to hear about Dad's life. My mom was not in the mood to do anything other than what was necessary.

My mother seemed unattached. She tried to look tough in her five-foot-and-four-inch tiny frame. She didn't cry, she didn't comfort her children, she just wanted to take care of business and move on. She had her head held high. She was not going to let any judgment get to her. She had a new life to run to when this was over, and this was just a necessary duty.

The cemetery was over thirty miles away in Buckeye. Dad was buried next to his father and brother. Mom asked me to find a ride to the cemetery because there was no room in her car to follow the hearse. I didn't think that would be a problem. Later I found out Carson was hiding in her car, and she just didn't want anyone to see him.

I went walking through the parking area of the church looking for Greg. He told me if he wasn't there, it was he couldn't get off work.

Almost everyone had left. Just then, my friend Nancy Gilkey rolled her window down and asked if I was okay. I said I needed a ride to Buckeye, and she asked me to hop in.

When we arrived at the cemetery, the dedicatory prayer had already started. Once that was over, they lowered the casket into the ground, and it was over. Mom said a quick good-bye to Jerry, Scott, and I, then left. She probably didn't want Carson to have to wait any longer being scrunched down in the backseat.

My grandma, aunts, and uncles from my dad's side were still there. They were sharing with me who was buried next to my dad. They shared with me that my dad's brother Terry also died of suicide. Once Mom left, they felt it was okay to talk to me. I am glad they did; I was worried they were mad at me.

I couldn't blame them for being upset. Mom excluded them from the funeral and any arrangements. They also knew Mom ran off with Carson, and that's what triggered Dad to kill himself.

Two days after the funeral, I returned to school, but the excitement of school and sports was gone. Thank goodness there was only four weeks left to summer break. My friends didn't know how to talk to me. Even the teachers seemed aloof. I was disappointed that the teachers didn't have something to say to me after having me for a student for several years in a small high school with only sixty-three students in my junior class. I think people were afraid to approach me, but I sure could have used a hug to two.

My friend Nancy came up and hugged me. "Welcome back," she said. Then she whispered in my ear, "Don't listen to any of the rumors."

Rumors, what rumors? What could anyone possibly have to say?

Nancy, whom we affectionately called Hank because of her cowgirl ways, told me there were stories about how my dad died, and she was there to defend me should I not want to deal with the stories.

I asked her, "What do you mean *how* he died?" I figured everyone knew by now it was suicide. She assured me I didn't need to worry and it was nobody's business. She rushed off to catch her class, but I was bewildered more than ever.

Later, I would find out that one of the students who was a known druggie (and a close friend of Carson's) was telling people that my dad was the target of a mafia hit because he was selling drugs from his place of business. My brother Scott told me about this rumor, and I immediately proved it false by dissecting the story: One, there is no mafia in Arizona. There are drug dealers and gangs, but no one refers to them as mafia. Two, I saw the hose and pillow on his truck seat. He did this to himself.

I asked Scott who he heard it from. He told me Mom and Carson told him. I couldn't believe what I was hearing. I knew why they told that lie: they didn't want to be responsible in, any way, for what happened to my dad. They were throwing suspicion off themselves. It was consistent with other lies the two of them had been telling to make themselves appear as victims in this mess rather than the reckless lovers that they were.

If people really wanted some juicy gossip, they could talk about how Posey Motors was across the alley from our backyard next to the bank. I don't think they knew our home was so close. The bank had repossessed Dad's one-year-old truck and had the dealership park it behind the business in the tow-yard area. The truck needed cleaning up with blood splattered all over the windows and the doors left open to air it out. We had full view of the truck. It was as if the bank was haunting us to have to see it every day for weeks. The student who was passing around rumors could have charged admission to view the truck; at least he would have evidence.

With each class, I just put my head down. I let the tears roll. I didn't want to think about anything anymore. My body would weep, and I would have no particular thoughts. I didn't know why I was crying, but that didn't matter. I had no resolve and nothing to look forward to.

Over the next few days, Jerry, Mom, and I had finished boxing up the house. I was hurt that Mom gave away all our possessions to anyone standing in line asking for them. She signed the house over to a local businessman. She didn't ask any one of her children if we wanted anything of our father's belongings to keep for a remembrance. As far as she was concerned, this life was yesterday's news.

A few months later, I was visiting my uncle Robert. He was wearing my dad's clothes. He asked if I wanted one of the coins from my dad's silver collection.

One? I thought to myself. How generous that he was offering me something that belonged to me to start with. In my grief and my need to have something of my father, I graciously accepted. I noticed he had my father's Bible with Dad's name embossed on the front of it. The Bible was a gift to our family from someone at church. I asked him if I could have it, and he didn't hesitate to give it to me.

I was miserable. I was also passive as a young girl and couldn't make any demands for information or help. I was fearful I would upset someone or seem disrespectful. I was so used to being in the shadows at home I just learned to keep quiet.

My head was spinning with all the uncertainty in my life. I missed my brother who left for military boot camp. I worried about Scott because I noticed he dropped out of school as a freshman and left town without a trace. I missed my younger siblings whom I was used to caring for every day. I just wanted our family to be together again, especially through this crisis. There was no one I could call to get any news, and Mom refused to give me her phone number.

I was holding out for the idea that someday, someday soon, we were all going to get back together. I kept telling myself this was just a temporary separation. I was good at absorbing all the pain rather than pushing it away. I just knew we would be back together soon if I would just be patient and faithful enough.

THE MESS GETS BIGGER

It's been three months now since Dad died. A family stepped forward and asked me if I wanted to live with them. I was thrilled to move in with them.

I had no choice but to move out from my grandma's place when an offer came to move in with another family. I struggled with loading up my few possessions I had in life now. It had only been a short time ago that I lost my father, was separated from my mother and siblings, and now I was being separated from my grandma.

I consoled myself that Grandma was only a few blocks away. I would stop and see her every day on my way home from school. Grandma Brown had lived with us throughout the years as a helper to my mother. She was my confidant and my caregiver for a long time. I felt loved by her. She had a gentleness that left me feeling like it was okay to be humble and submissive; I felt like the world needed more people who were tender and subservient and the world needed more love and kindness. I wanted to be just like her.

Grandma made life interesting. I admired her ability to find beauty in simple things, like her poetry and art paintings. She would save up extra sugar from her free food from the church so she could buy a small can of cocoa and make fudge for Christmas presents. She would save her round oatmeal containers and paint the boxes black with her art supplies to put the fudge in. She would talk to you as if you were the only person in the world, and she had nothing more important to do other than to listen to you answer all her questions.

Once, when I was about nine years old, she was getting ready to take us kids to a midday church activity that was on the other side of Tucson. She needed to buy gas first. On our way to church that day, before we stopped for gas, our red station wagon stalled on the railroad tracks from lack of gas. It was a large crossing. There were five tracks to cross. The lights and bells went off, and the bars were coming down. A train was blowing its horn at us to move. Grandma was panic-stricken. There were five of us small children in that car with her. The car wouldn't turn over, it was out of gas, and a train was coming. She folded her arms and started to pray. Just then, the train passed in front of the car going very fast, and you could feel the car rattling. The noise was so loud that we grabbed our ears to stop the pain.

"Grandma! What do we do?" I screamed over the noise.

"Nothing," she said as she shook her head no. I wondered if we were supposed to open the door and run. It missed us by inches. Had we stalled a few more inches forward, we would have been smashed to pieces.

As a child, I truly believed it was her prayer that kept us safe; as an adult, I realized we probably got lucky on this one. As a child, I watched her show faith on many occasions, and I was determined that I wanted to tap into that same power.

I did not want to stop living with her. At the time, she was my main source of love. Her words to me as I left her were, "Until you have a testimony of the gospel, you can borrow mine." Those words would sear into my memory. I did borrow hers; I couldn't have done well without it. *I needed to pull down the power of heaven more than ever, now.*

I loved the new family I moved in with. The Hopkins owned a local cement plant outside of town. It was a relief not to be a financial burden on them.

They had two daughters, Diana and Carolyn. Diana was my age. We knew each other at school because it was just a small town, but we had not been together in our activities to get to know each other better. Carolyn was two years younger than me, and I think it was a little unsettling to her to have to share her family with a stranger. She was nice to me, but I could sense she was irritated with me at times and wished I wasn't there. I could understand. It is difficult to share your home with strangers.

Jack was a great dad. He was a gentle man who seemed to always have kind words of encouragement for all us teenage girls. He was exactly the opposite of my dad. He spoke lovingly toward his girls, and he never raised his voice or hit them.

Diane was an incredible mom. Her name was the same as the daughter's name except one had an *a* and one had an *e*. She made dinner every day, and she did all the laundry. I remembered being so embarrassed when I came home one day to find my underwear folded neatly on the dryer. I didn't want anyone to see my underwear!

Besides, in my family, I was the one who did the laundry. I had some adjusting to do.

Diane was gentle in nature too. She spoke softly, and she did all the household chores without any help from us. I felt out of place not having to2 do chores. She also helped Jack with his business doing the accounting. She did all she could to encourage her daughters and made them feel accepted and special.

I was still dating Greg. Jack and Diane had no problem with me dating like my parents did. Greg was a lifesaver. I looked forward to his evening visits after work. I loved that we never fought and he was a gentleman around me.

Greg and I were immediately attracted to each other the first time we met at church. It was shortly after I moved to Gila Bend at the age of fourteen. He had brownish-blond hair, parted on the side, as a young boy would comb it. When he smiled at me, his cheeks flushed, and then he would look down at the ground. He was cute but a little shy. He was eighteen at the time, and that was just too old for my parents to accept, so we kept our attraction in the shadows. He also had a girlfriend that he had dated through high school, so we settled on being secret friends.

During our friendship era, he would drive by my family's trailer and rev up his engine to let me know he was passing by on his way to the recreation center, and I would drop whatever I was doing to meet him at the recreation center at the center of the trailer park. I would tell my parents I was going over to play pool or air hockey and would be home soon.

The attraction between the two of us was obvious. We sparred with each other in a competitive way, and yet we acted as if the jury was out with a decision as to whether we liked each other or not. Greg and I would flirt shamelessly and bump into each other all the while knowing that we were innocent of any wrongdoing. He would bring his friend Martin with him to the recreation center at times so we would never be caught being alone.

During my first year with Greg, I would have other temporary boyfriend crushes, but eventually I would find myself charmed by Greg's attention and meeting up with him at the recreation center, going four-wheeling in his truck or meeting up after church. He was always a gentleman so I trusted him and enjoyed many outings without fear of any commitment.

After secretly dating for a year, things changed. After sneaking around his girlfriend, Cathy, he finally broke up with her. Greg drove to my house and asked me to sit in his truck next to him; he had something he wanted to tell me.

"When does your dad get home?" he asked quietly.

"I'm not sure, maybe in an hour or two," I said, understanding why he was asking. Greg could not be at my house when my dad got home, or we would both get yelled at. My mom and dad were adamantly against my seeing a much older boy.

He sat in the driver seat, put his arm around me, and stared into my eyes. I really felt uncomfortable but defiant at the same time. We could flirt and talk, but Greg had never tried to be serious with me.

What was he going to say to me that I didn't already know? He reached over and kissed me.

I was shocked. I didn't expect that. We were both so good at playing the role of friend for so long, this was the last thing I expected. *Wait, what does that kiss mean?* I couldn't think fast enough what was happening to me.

I had no time to think as he pulled me closer and went for another short, passionate kiss.

He stopped long enough to look at me seriously and utter the words, "I love you."

I couldn't help it, I started to giggle. I don't know why I couldn't be serious for the moment, but it was all such a change in direction from where we had been, and I was a little embarrassed. I had never been kissed like that! I was only fifteen at the time.

I could see his countenance drop a little that I wasn't being as serious as he was. Oh, I had always wanted Greg for a boyfriend, but I had settled long ago for being the secret, good friend. I needed more time to assess what was happening. By the end of the day, I had the boyfriend I always wanted, and I was in love back.

We dated steadily for about a year. He was a bright spot in my life because my father ruled with an iron fist, and Greg was the opposite. He was gentle and kind. My mother made me the housekeeper, cook, and babysitter since I was the oldest daughter; so being with Greg meant freedom. I could stay a little longer at school after cheer and sports practice to visit Greg before heading home, and my parents would never know.

One year the rodeo was in town, and Greg was going to ride a bull! I was so excited; I got all cleaned up and put on my cute polyester mint-green cowgirl pants with some really cute cowboy boots that belonged to my mother.

Just as I was about the leave the house, my dad asked where I was going. I said I was going to the rodeo, not thinking that was a problem as my brothers were already at the rodeo.

Dad said, "No, you are not going. Have you done the laundry yet?"

The laundry? I said to myself in exasperation. *That will take hours to finish!* I decided I would not cry or argue. I would just go start the laundry. I was spineless. I put one load in and took the other six loads and shoved them under my bed.

As soon as one load was finished (mostly Dad's clothes), I folded them and put them on his bed. I didn't put them away as I wanted him to see them. I snuck off to the rodeo and had a great time cheering Greg on. Dad never knew about the other six loads.

Greg pampered me. He would take me to my first movie in a theater. He would take me to my first sit-down restaurant. He was loyal, safe to be with, funny, and spiritual—everything I needed and wanted for my first love. I grew dependent on him. He was the prince that would rescue this Cinderella.

We met two years before, and it seemed like we were always together. Two months after my father died, Greg took me on a drive down Watermelon Road outside of town. He stopped at one of the side roads going into a cotton field.

"I hate seeing you like this. I wish I could help you more. I don't like seeing you cry, I don't know what to do for you. I really want to help take care of you. Maybe we should get married?" he said.

I always thought I would marry Greg someday, but this just seemed so out of place.

"I can't get married while I am still in high school!" I blurted it out and watched his face sadden with disappointment in me. I think I left him with the feeling that he wasn't good enough to rescue me. I wish I could take back my quick impulse. I needed to say it though.

I wouldn't say no, but I couldn't say yes. We would leave it open ended for a later discussion. I was still a senior in high school, and I just needed to finish that chapter of my life.

A few nights after Greg's proposition, I was tossing and turning, finding it difficult to fall asleep. I had been crying while trying to sleep. I felt despair. I was still having immense loneliness and sadness for my family. It was around midnight, and I decided to get up and go for a walk in the desert.

The moon was full, and the dirt road was lit up as if it were almost daylight. I felt as if my footsteps were being guided.

I walked about a mile thinking about the losses I was experiencing. I was in a lot of pain. I rarely could think about my situation without tears flooding down my cheeks. I could talk to myself, but that wasn't always helpful. I was unable to comfort myself most of the time because I did not have something to look forward to about my family. I finally fell to my knees, sobbing and pleading with my Heavenly Father to help me.

I didn't know what I should do with my life. I didn't know how to make the pain stop. I didn't know how to stop feeling so lonely without my family around. I was blank inside, and I felt depressed. I even asked what I should do about Greg and his marriage proposal. I don't know where that came from; it just slipped out.

I didn't receive any direct revelation. I just got up and felt this great peace come over me. There were no more tears, and I sang songs all the way back. I was unaware that my life would change drastically from that moment on.

About a week later, Greg did not come to visit me after work like what he usually does every night for the last year. I left him phone messages, but no response. The second night, he didn't come by. I made mention of it to my close friend, Susie. She was dating Henry who was Greg's best friend. She told me she didn't want to be the one to tell me but that she heard Greg met another girl in Buckeye.

No way, absolutely no way Greg would ever do that to me, I thought to myself.

The third night, he didn't show up. I thought I would drive over to Buckeye, a small town about thirty miles away, and cruise around Main Street to see if I could find Greg's truck. It was a small town, and if he were out running around, there was a chance I would run into him. After a few hours, I gave up and just went to his parents' house back in Gila Bend. I sat in his driveway until he came home around midnight.

He was shocked to see me there. I asked him where he had been and why he didn't return my phone calls. He went off about a late dentist appointment, how he had not been home to return the calls, and how he had been working late.

I stopped him with his excuses and said sternly, "Where have you been tonight?"

"Buckeye."

"No you weren't, I was there driving around looking for you."

His face pulled back in shock and he said, "You were?"

Then tearfully I said, "Tell me now where you have been, or I will drive away and never speak to you again."

Now he had tears swelled up in his eyes. He looked at me, hesitated, and said, "I can't, it will hurt you."

I repeated it slowly, holding back the tears as I gritted my teeth, "Tell me where you have been."

He lowered his voice and looked to the ground. "I can't."

I put my car in gear and told him I meant what I said, and I would never speak to him again. I drove off, barely able to breathe. I screamed again and again and again. The pain would engulf me. It was true—he met another girl.

I was devastated. I had lost everything at this point. I went home and slept on the couch. I shared a room with Diana, and I didn't want to wake her up with my crying noises. I woke up the next morning to Carolyn talking on the phone in the kitchen.

"She doesn't look good, Mom," Carolyn was trying to speak softly, but I could hear her.

"Things don't look good," Carolyn said. I was pretty sure she was reporting in to her mom at work. They must have heard me sobbing most of the night on the couch.

I stopped eating for about five days and was numb with pain. I was living in a semi comatose state while in school. I would lie on the couch every evening staring at the ceiling, wondering if it were possible to hold my breath and make my breathing stop for good.

I just wanted to die. I thought I was in pain when my dad died and my mother left, but this was the world crashing down on me, full weight bearing, crushing me to powder. *How could I end my life? How could I stop all of this pain?* I would imagine myself driving into oncoming traffic. It had been months of pain piling up and buckets of tears flowing down. *How do you stop living? I just wanted to stop living!*

Greg tried to call me a few times, but I asked the Hopkins not to call me to the phone if he called. I didn't want to talk to him. I missed him, but I could never be cheated on—never. My trust switch was broken from the abandonment of my parents. Little did I realize how much impact this would have on future relationships and, eventually, my marriage.

One night, Greg did come by the house and ask to talk to me. We sat in his truck under the carport. He started to tell me he wasn't sure he wanted to marry Tracy, I was numb. I just stared at the dashboard. I didn't even want to hear her name or even talk about her. For sure, my attraction to him was gone after hearing him speak her name.

I didn't want to be a second choice—ever. No matter how much it hurt, I wasn't coming back. No matter how much I needed him in my life again, I couldn't bring myself to do it. I just went into my submissive self, asked to get out of the truck, and returned to the house speechless. I couldn't even tell him off.

A few days later, I saw him driving toward me on Main Street. My heart jumped with pain, for a moment, being reminded that we were no longer together. Within few seconds, I could see him behind the driver's wheel and for the first time saw his new girlfriend sitting next to him. I was crushed all over again.

I went into a fit of rage, screaming in pain. The rage was clashing with my tears. *I don't want to live anymore! I am done! I can't keep doing this!* I screamed in at the top of my lungs, "Why? Why? Why?" I immediately took a side street so he couldn't see my red, swollen face.

Within four months, Greg was married. There could be no more hanging on. That door was shut. What made it worse was that eventually he and his new wife moved onto the same street as the Hopkins. I couldn't even describe the shock and anguish I was in.

I had brought an orange tabby kitten from Grandma's that I befriended with me to the Hopkins. I named it Jake, after Greg's nickname about his last name. One day, a small rainstorm was passing through, and a well-meaning neighbor noticed my car window slightly rolled down. They stopped and rolled it up without noticing my kitten was asleep on the seat. In the Arizona heat, it only takes a few hours to die in a car with no ventilation, and the kitten died. I was starting to feel like everything in my life was cursed.

Greg and Tracy seemed to be everywhere: I would see them in the stands at football games I was cheer-leading at. His truck would be on Main Street and I would have to take a side street to avoid seeing him. I stopped going to church to avoid seeing them.

One time, Greg had the nerve to pull in behind me after seeing me ditch him behind the bank. He got out of his car and walked over to my window.

"I hear you are racing your car out at the old airstrip, is that true? I'm concerned and worried about you," he asked.

"Yep, that's me, and yes, I was with your buddies, and no, it is none of your business. Don't ever talk to me again!" I shot back. Then I hit the gas, and the car shot forward, leaving him to step out of the way of flying dirt and rocks.

I could have puked hearing him say he was worried about me. If he was so worried about me or had so much concern about me, maybe he should not have hurt me.

A few months later, after a football game, a few of us were cruising along Main Street and hang out at the Dairy Queen. I was laughing with my friends, and we were feeling crazy about winning the game and playing chase in the cars. Out of nowhere, Greg's wife, Tracy, drove up next me in the other lane and flipped me off.

What? What did I ever do to her to cause this random act of insanity? She won! I didn't fight for him! He is hers!

My friends didn't take it lightly. Angie told me to pull over as she wanted to drive. As soon as she was in the driver's seat, she peeled out to chase Tracy down for flipping me off.

Angie rolled her window down and yelled out. "Pull over, Tracy." I was petrified. I didn't want to start any trouble. I was even more shocked when Tracy pulled over on Martin Street just before the railroad tracks!

I kept saying, "No no no! Angie, leave her alone."

Angie assured me she wasn't going to hurt her as she jumped out of the car and went up to Tracy's window.

"Why did you do that?" Angie yelled through the window crack, standing over Tracy's door.

Tracy rolled the window down a little more and said, "I don't know why I did that, I'm sorry."

Angie was from Florida and had a thick Southern accent, and all of us in the car who were watching roared with laughter when she said, "You better be sorry. You should be acting like a married woman, not some immature jerk!"

Angie marched back to my car, got in the driver's seat, and pulled away. I was stunned, but a little happy. I had the best friends anyone could ask for that night. I felt like someone was in my corner, even if it were just for one night.

I was halfway through the school year. My life in this small town was going to come to an end soon. I just needed to hang on for a little longer.

A Season of Awareness

Living with the Hopkins during my senior year was quite different than the way I was raised. It was good for me to see how family members interact with one another. It was good for me to see how Jack and Diane would work together. I really liked how they treated us girls; it was the perfect balance of time and money.

Diane bought me a real gold-chain bracelet, and it was the first piece of jewelry I had ever owned. For graduation, I received a beautiful watch. I felt pretty, loved, and included.

Diane even took me on the family vacation to Seattle. I experienced being on a plane for the first time. I was amazed with the tall pine trees and constant rain. Everything was green and lush. I had not been outside of Arizona since the age of five, and the dry desert was my only experience for landscaping.

Diane not only went to her daughter's activities, but she also went to mine. One time she was at one of my softball games, and I heard her voice cheering behind the fence. I turned around and asked her, "What are you doing here?"

She was puzzled at my question. "I'm here to watch you play," she said.

Now, I was puzzled. Neither of my parents had ever been to one of my high school volleyball, softball, or basketball games—ever.

I tried to keep busy after school with sports, and I worked on the weekends at the local café, the Best Western Space Age Lodge, for gas money for my car.

I was invited once to go clothes shopping with them. I felt so ashamed to make the comment that I had no money. I usually had a little, but I was broke this week. Diane had no problem giving me one hundred dollars to go with them. This was definitely a change from my parents.

I wasn't sure how I was supposed to feel about Diane being so generous. I got into an argument once with my dad when I was a sophomore because I needed money for school pictures. He refused to give it to me, yet my oldest brother, Jerry, seemed to have everything he needed. He had a car, new clothes, and spending money. I had not asked for money from my parents before those school pictures, and I was told no! I was so angry I went and got a job at the A&W Root Beer stand as a cashier and refused to ask my parents for money again. Now, Diane was freely giving me money, no strings attached, and I was overwhelmed with her generosity. Diane was always on the front lines for me. When the school called and was making a fuss over my living with a family that was not my legal guardian, she stood up and went to fight for me. I really thought I was going to have to move in again with my mom, and it was unsettling to me. I cried after hanging up the phone to the school.

"Why does everything bad happen to me?" I said in exasperation.

She was a little stern with me and said, "*We* happened to you, and that's not bad."

I had to stop crying. She was right. As a teenager, everything felt like drama, drama, drama. There wasn't a better place for me to be at this time than with them. I will be forever grateful for their generosity. I learned that living with them made a huge impact on me when raising my own children. I had a pattern I could follow. I don't think they knew just how significant their influence was.

I started to realize that even in my darkest hour of loneliness, I was in some ways getting a new chance at life. I was no longer bound to the house with cleaning, cooking, and babysitting for my younger siblings day after day. I was no longer at the mercy of my parents' whims whether I could leave the house or not. I didn't have to resent not having money for basic things. I didn't have to worry about covering bruises from the beatings with a belt or a stick. I was finally wearing clothes that were not hand-me-down jeans and T-shirts from my brother. There were three meals a day now living with the Hopkins, and the fear of making a parent angry was gone.

I was involved in drama, art, sports and cheerleading so I had plenty of activities to keep me active; however, I had changed. I was no longer a happy teenager. The next dance, new dress, or game meant nothing to me anymore. The excitement was gone, and to make matters worse, I couldn't stop thinking about Greg.

I was broken inside. I couldn't trust anyone with my emotions. I admit, I was emotionally needy. I cried unexpectedly at times. I did not want to date anyone or hang out with friends. I felt like a wedge between me and the rest of my friends because of these despondent feelings. I was being talked about at school, and I knew it. I didn't care. I was probably an emotionally needy mess to others, and that wasn't cool. I just needed to finish school and leave this small town. There was absolutely nothing left for me here.

Although I lamented my family situation, Scott, Kristen, and Terry had things much worse. Mom and Carson were living their lives like two high school druggies who were always looking forward to their next high. They kept skipping to different towns, moving every few months because they didn't want to pay the bills as they would pile up. Scott was in and out of their home frequently as he was old enough to challenge Carson, and when Carson drank, he became violent. Mom and Carson kept kicking Scott out. There was too much exposure to alcohol and drugs to Scott, Kristen, and Terry. The exposure to this environment would nearly ensure they would make those same choices as they were entering their junior high years.

Things did not get better between me and my mom. She was hostile and indifferent toward me when she would call me. When I talked to her, she didn't make sense, she couldn't stay focused, and her emotions would change drastically in the same sentence.

One time I called Mom because I had decided to go to college after high school graduation, but I needed the social security check that was in my name to be sent to me.

"If you want to come live with us, I can show you where the money is being spent. I will not send you any money. We need it here," she told me.

"Mom, my portion of the social security check will stop going to you anyhow if I do not go to college. I can't go to college without it," I pleaded.

"I just need you to sign over my portion when I leave for college, and you can continue to keep my portion for this current school year," I begged. She still refused.

She was so angry with me for asking for my portion.

"If you had been half the daughter you should have been, maybe your father would not have killed himself," she said in a nasty tone.

"You don't mean that."

"Yes, I do."

I could tell the conversation needed to end. She was threatened by the change of money and wanted to strike back at me.

Later, I had Diane take me to the Social Security office and asked them to send my portion of the check to me after I graduated from high school.

After Mom's comment blaming me for Dad's death, for sure I would not move in with her. I could see how dangerous and toxic that would be. High school had lost its savor. I had a few weeks to finish, but it was crawling. I was busy, but I was more concerned about what I would do after high school and how could I get out of this town. Besides, I couldn't stand to be around Carson. No matter how friendly and accepting he was of me, he was not my father, and was not going to replace my father.

In fact, he was the man responsible for our family's breakup. Mom was drinking heavily now and behaving in the most bizarre ways. There was no way I wanted to be near any of that. It was obvious to me that we were not going to get back together as a family as she chose Carson over her children.

I did spend Christmas that year with her and Carson and my siblings in New Mexico. It felt so good to be around my siblings. It felt so good to see everyone happy to see me. I cried a little inside, but I had to be strong for them. I wanted to be the older sister who kept things positive and fun. Jerry was the only one missing. He was stationed in Germany.

Carson kept his distance. He didn't want to interfere with my relationship with my family. He didn't talk much except to tell wild, tall tales of his exploits that he thought would endear me to him. It didn't work. I was reluctant to be cold or mean to him because I didn't want to sever the relationship with my mother or my siblings for future reunions. I just kept things to myself. This would be one of the last times we would be all together.

I was a little surprised to discover that I worried myself sick about my mom and siblings when I was away from them, and in return, none of them worried about me. Everyone thought I was fine and that I didn't need them. Nothing could have been farther from the truth.

Five months later, graduation night had finally come. I was so excited. My mom said she would come to see me. I couldn't wait! I was going to see my siblings and give them a big hug from their big sister. I looked and looked all night in the stands, hoping they were just late. I couldn't find them anywhere. I had talked to my mom earlier in the day when she phoned me that she made it to town. I knew for sure she was going to be there.

She never did show up. After the ceremony, everyone gathered onto the football field to be with their graduate, and there I stood, one more time, all by myself. All I could think was, *Why didn't I just stay home?* I don't know why I thought she would show; she missed all my school activities this year when she only lived two hours away. I just didn't want to believe she would miss my graduation, too.

James, one of my cousins from my dad's side, about ten years old, ran up to me with a box and said, "This is from Grandma Martin." And he ran off. I wish I could have found my mom as I really felt stupid standing there alone. I looked around for the Hopkins and couldn't find them either.

I opened the box and found a beautiful, hand-sewn quilt in the box. There were pink and blue squares on one side and a toile print on the other. The most important thing to me that night was that my grandma Martin was thinking of me. It saved me from feeling like the most forgotten person in the world that night.

It would be months later that I would have the chance to ask my mother why she didn't show up for graduation when she was in town.

She couldn't remember why she didn't make it. She said she must have gotten busy and forgot. I found out later that she was at a local tavern and had too much to drink to be in public. The person who told me said I would have been embarrassed if she had shown up.

I started to recognize that I couldn't rely on Mom for anything. If I could find a way to take care of myself and stay in college, I would be free of the insecurity of taking care of myself. I would have the strength I needed to stand on my own. I could be in an environment free from exposure to substance abuse and trashy conversation that was prevalent in my mother's home.

However, as a teenager, no matter how much I wanted to be angry with Mom and Carson, I had a strong feeling not to get angry; if I did, they would win and would have control over me emotionally. As long as I did not allow them to affect my emotions, I could not be sucked in to their crazy world of drugs, alcohol, stealing, and promiscuity. I would not let them have any influence over me—ever.

I distinctly remember having a great sense of empathy for my mother. If I was suffering, she must be too. There had to be guilt that she was dealing with as well, but in conversations with her later in life, she didn't feel any guilt, and what I couldn't understand was her lack of concern for me.

I was given the book *Without Conscience* by Robert D. Hare in my adult years. It points out that many people have different levels of psychosis, and our prisons are filled with people who believe their own lies and have little concern for others besides themselves because of mental illness.

The book explained how people have different levels of psychosis and are master manipulators because they do not have the same conscience that normal people would. The sociopathic person lives to fulfill their own desires and has little regard for how others might feel. These individuals are also the ones who will kill the family cat as a prank and think nothing of it. These individuals as the book points out are "without conscience."

Once I read the book, I reflected back on my childhood and it all made sense now. Meals were not as consistent and workloads became unbearable for me. When Grandma wasn't with us, things would get worse for us kids.

As a young child, this was excruciating. We often did chores through breakfast and lunch and gave up Saturday-morning cartoons and playtime. We certainly couldn't have friends over or go outside and play with the neighborhood kids who gathered in the street for games.

We were yelled at, pushed, hit, and put on restriction if we did not keep up with Mom's frantic pace. The last thing we wanted was to have Mom mad at us because hours later when Dad got home, and everyone had forgot what she was mad about to begin with, she would point to whichever child she wanted to have the belt beating, and Dad would take care of it right then and there without question. I have to ask myself this over and over as an adult: Why did I miss my family so much as a teen?

The constant fear of beatings and heavy workloads, being free would be preferred.

Then I realized that no matter how bad your family is, as a child that is all you know. You are wired to love your parents. You don't even know if their behavior is right or wrong, because you are programmed to trust them to take care of you. You trust them to protect you and love you. Most of the time, you accept this is how your parents love you.

As time went on, I became aware that God left messages for me in dreams. I would go on to have more dreams, and they would become pivotal in my decisions. Looking back, I discovered that God was mindful of what I was going through or about to go through because of the dreams I had.

I had a vivid dream when I was about eight years old. I dreamed that someone I knew put me in the trunk of a car. I was frightened, but not too frightened, as I knew who that person was and didn't think they would hurt me. I was excited when the trunk was starting to open to let me out. However, instead of helping me out, the person stabbed me in the stomach with a knife and shut the trunk again.

I remember the horrifying feeling of my trust being violated by someone who was supposed to love me as I writhed in pain. I have had several occasions to relive that feeling when dealing with my mother. I believe now the dream was a forewarning. Although I couldn't make sense of it, I distinctly remember the feelings I had, and nothing else in my life has caused me to have those same feelings except in dealing with my mother.

A Season of Peace

High school was over, and I was on my way to Utah. My cousin Sheri who was living in Utah called me just before graduation and invited me to come live with her when I finished high school.

Heck, why not go to college in Utah? Where else do I have to go?

This was a defining moment for me. I wanted so badly to break the grip of fear that if I didn't go to college, I would have to move in with my mom. I had also received a six-hundred-dollar scholarship from the local Lions Club, and that was a motivation for me to at least try college.

I knew that if I could get my social security money, some grant money, and a job, I could make this happen. As it turned out, I qualified for the maximum Pell Grant benefit, and I was able to get a job on campus. I felt powerful. I knew I could change the outcome of my life by going to college.

I was excited to go live with my cousin. Sheri and I spent two weeks every summer together that I can remember growing up. She was two years older than me, and we were close friends. I could trust her, and I knew for sure I would have a lot of fun around her.

Although it had been several years since I had seen her, my mind flooded with memories of our childhood activities together. In particular was the last summer I spent with her when I was fourteen. We went with her parents camping up in the White Mountains for a month. We had time to fish, build small dams in the stream, catch garden snakes as they warmed up in the sun, catch frogs, trade beer for horse rides with some Indians on the reservation, and live life as though all that was important was the next adventure we could conjure up.

Now, if you asked others who were camping next to us, you might have a different story. Sheri was a prankster. She was bold and daring compared to my submissive personality; I was just the sidekick, trusting we would never get hurt or get arrested. I couldn't resist going back in time with my thoughts; it was as if the details were etched in my mind.

"Sheri, stop!" I screamed as she was taunting me with the frog she had just captured with her hands. We had been catching snakes too. I had dreams of taking them home and making them pets. Sheri wanted to drop the frog in boiling water to see if it would jump out.

"I just want to see if it will jump out," she continued. "What do you think it will do? Jump out or die?"

I didn't want to know because there was a chance it would die. I got squeamish and closed my eyes. She dropped the frog in, and no, it didn't jump out. It took one last stretch and died. I was sad inside. I wasn't the type of person who could handle cruelty in any way.

Sheri, kind of, giggled in embarrassment. "I didn't think it would die. Now we know," she said.

Sheri put the snake that we caught inside someone's jean pocket while they were using the showers. The three-hundred-pound gentleman almost had a heart attack when he got dressed.

When we traded Sheri's dad's beer with the Indians, Sheri started talking to me in pig Latin every time they started talking in Apache, so they thought we were negotiating among ourselves just like they were.

"Oday ouya inkthay eythay nowknay atwhay eway are ayinsay?" Sheri was proficient in pig Latin. It is a made-up language taking the first letter of each word and moving it to the end of the word and adding *ay*. For instance, *inkthay* is "think." She was asking me, "Do you think they know what we are saying?"

We ended up with two horses for two hours in exchange for two beers.

The dam we built in the stream was to get all the fish for ourselves and not let the other campers downstream catch any for a few days. Finally, her cousin Kenny came to visit for a few days. When he would set our alarm for three in the morning as a joke, Sheri spied him and invited him over for ex-lax hot chocolate the next night. He spent the next day at the outhouse. His mother almost had a stroke letting us know what she thought of us.

Yep, going to live with Sheri in Utah was going to be fun. I could use some fun.

We left for Utah the day after high school graduation. It was a twelve-hour drive from Arizona to Utah. Mrs. Hopkins and her oldest daughter, Diana, drove it in one day to Sheri's in Manti, Utah. They dropped me off at the house in Utah, and in less than ten minutes, they were back in the car driving back toward Arizona.

I can't blame them for wanting to leave so quickly. The house Sheri and my aunt Nancy were staying in was a turn-of-the-century, mouse-infested, dilapidated mess with a woodstove that needed fed constantly and stunk up the whole house with the smell of smoke. I could understand Mrs. Hopkins not wanting to stay the night. To me it was heavenly because I was home; I was with family.

"Sheri!" I exclaimed.

"Shelly!" She squealed back, and we embraced for a hug. Then I made my way to my aunt Nancy to hug her. The room was warm from the fire burning, and a world of familiarity and love just came over me like a warm blanket.

My cousin Sheri was also living with her ten-year old brother, Johnny. Aunt Nancy (who was my mother's sister) had just been through an ugly divorce too, and that was what caused her to move away from Arizona. What a fine bunch we were, all three of us with broken hearts and empty wallets.

Sheri and Nancy had just moved there in the last year. Aunt Nancy had six dollars left in her pocket when she arrived. Aunt Nancy had a friend from Ajo, Arizona, who moved to Utah and told her it was a wonderful place to start a new life.

Their neighbors wasted no time in welcoming them to the neighborhood. When they discovered the bleakness of Nancy's situation, the man who owned the home told them they could live there rent-free for six months.

The other neighbors came over and tilled the backyard area and handed them a bunch of packet seeds and told them to get busy; the planting season was almost over. The local church helped them to get a food order and some wood for the fireplace. Although times were going to be tough, there were good people ready to help them and support them where necessary to give them a hand up, but not a handout.

My aunt Nancy was an extension of my grandma Brown. Aunt Nancy had lived through the poverty years in Nebraska with my mother as a young girl. Aunt Nancy had the unconditional love my grandma had. I loved to be around my aunt Nancy. She giggled a lot and was like Grandma when it came to looking for the good in people and praising God regardless of the circumstances. You just felt accepted when you are around her. Grandma and I would continue to write each other, but now I had another angel in my life.

Aunt Nancy would tell me stories about Grandma. Grandma seemed to always have faith. It was all she had in life. Her life was exceptionally hard growing up; losing both her parents very early, she was sent to live with her grandparents and then in a sanatorium as a teen for a lung problem. All she ever knew was extreme poverty. Her first husband abandoned her with two young daughters for a mistress. Her second husband would also abandon her with three additional children, one of them handicapped. My mother was in the second set of children. They lived in an abandoned railroad boxcar in Nebraska. There was no running water or electricity to the boxcar. The one-room shanty Grandma was living in now must have been heaven compared to what she had lived in before.

My aunt would tell me stories of how they would steal chickens from neighboring farms and steal milk off porch steps to survive. My grandmother would praise God despite the poverty, loss, and abuse from men in her life. She always looked for the good around her even though her burdens were heavy.

Once my grandmother moved her three young children to Arizona from Nebraska to live with one of her older daughters, the situation started to improve; however, it didn't surprise me that my own mother got married at fifteen to escape it all. Aunt Nancy married at fourteen. She had two small children when she left her cheating husband and married his older brother; she had two more children and was living in Ajo, Arizona, owning a home, having a husband who worked in the copper mines, a car, and an account at the company store. There was no more poverty for her.

This all happened a few years ago during Sheri's last year of high school back in Arizona. She married her boyfriend with the promises of him taking care of her only to discover quickly that he had a bad temper and violent disposition. Sheri would leave him within the year and join her mother in Utah. There we were, the three of us, looking for a fresh start in life in the obscure, tiny town of Manti.

Manti, Utah, was a charming town. It was small with a population of about three thousand people, had a Main Street, it was clean, and filled with religious history and a distinct culture. It was certainly a contrast to the dry desert of Arizona. Utah had large and leafy trees everywhere, green grass for lawns, and mile after mile of green fields, with lots of large mountains and hills from one end of the state to the other.

As charming as the small town of Manti was, it had very few jobs to offer. It was ninety minutes north to the larger city of Provo. It was a farming community, and Sheri and I wasted no time in exploring.

On my first day there, Sheri took me to a turkey farm. I had never seen the likes of thousands of turkeys fenced in making a constant gobbling sound. She pulled up to the farm's fence in her mom's 1960-something car that seemed to require a quart of oil a day. We got out of the car, she beat the door panel with her palm, and she yelled loudly at the turkeys, "Hey, everybody, Shelly's here!"

At that very moment, thousands of turkeys came running over to us. The turkey's gobbling got louder and louder. I think they thought she was going to feed them. I looked around quickly to see if anyone was looking, and then I looked at Sheri. While embarrassed and laughing, I said, "Stop it! Just stop it! They don't know who I am."

She said, "See, even the turkeys are happy you are here!"

And a warm welcome it was! I just looked at Sheri in amazement. She always knew how to make me laugh.

We went to dances at the tennis courts every Friday night. The main event in that small town was cruising in a car up and down the Main Street and sometimes having water-balloon fights from the other cars and trucks.

It was fun until someone started using buckets of water after convincing us to roll our windows down to talk.

Sheri had long, beautiful, blond hair. She was cute, thin, and funny. I was the "wingman" as some would say. She was the magnet that could attract all the attention we ever needed. One night we drove the ninety minutes to Provo and went to a disco tech for dancing. While we were there, two foreigners from the Middle East came up and asked us both to dance. By the time we were back to our table, Sheri had told a huge story to these guys that we were dancers with *Donny & Marie* as ice skaters.

I couldn't believe she was telling this story, with lots of details that weren't true. It was hard to keep a straight face. Sheri was trying hard to get me to laugh. She had a great imagination. She said that's what they get for asking if we were professional dancers because we danced so well. She also thought it would give them bragging rights back home, and it was harmless because we would never see them again.

We would spend our days at Palisades Lake sun bathing, we would hike up into Manti Canyon, and we would go from town to town for the summer festivals and holiday celebrations. Sheri was mischievous, and I was delighted in whatever she had up her sleeve next.

Even with all the fun, I needed to work to survive. After a month of checking every possible lead, Sheri and I landed a job at the Pacific Trails sewing plant.

For Sheri, this job was perfect. She was an excellent seamstress. She was talented with sewing her own clothing and prom dresses.

She was immediately put on the fast machines and higher-piece–rate chart. Me, I could barely keep my machine from jamming, so they moved me to sorting and packing.

Sheri would put a piece of toilet paper at the top of her spool as a flag to signal me to take a restroom break. We would take a break at the same time.

We would chatter and make jokes about what we were doing and laugh about the crazy ladies we worked with. It was the perfect rest from what seemed like a long day's work for about $3.75 an hour. College would start in about two months. I could do anything for that long. I realized this job was hard work for what little money I made! Surely college would save me.

Neither of us was much interested in local relationships then. I was too busy trying to let my heart heal, and Sheri was in a long-distance relationship with Roger, a football player, who went home from the local college for the summer.

We enrolled at Snow College, the local junior college about five miles away, in Ephraim. Unfortunately for me, Roger wasn't coming back to Snow. He wanted to get married to Sheri before school started and live in Wyoming. I was the odd man out.

There I was, alone again. This time I was in a community that I had no connections with and, in the middle of nowhere, surrounded by numerous turkey farms. Looking back, it was safe, and it was perfect for getting educated without a lot of distractions. This was exactly where a young girl who was on her own needed to be.

School started, and there was a moment when I thought everything was going along fine until I received a phone call from Sheri. Grandma had died of a heart attack; now I needed to go back to Arizona for the funeral.

I wailed with pain. I couldn't take much more. I needed her more than ever in my life, and now God had removed my most reliable source of love. I cried all the way to Arizona. Although I had little money for gas and food, I wouldn't miss her funeral for anything.

The loneliness was starting to consume me. As usual, I was having a hard time asking anyone for help emotionally. I just wanted to be strong inside, but I didn't know how. I just wanted to hold out and not give up on the idea that my family was going to be together soon.

I would keep telling myself, *As soon as Mom comes around and changes her mind about Carson.*

Mom never came around, and my mom didn't even attend her own mother's funeral.

I was in my thirties before I realized God took my grandma when he did because she could help me from the other side far more than she could here. She would be in my dreams giving me guidance and bringing me comfort. She could help me from the other side without the constraints of poverty. She could prepare me for what was still to come.

School started. I really didn't fit in. I got into an argument with my roommates because they thought I was using their toothpaste and shampoo. They noticed I was out of mine. I lived from a monthly social security check and was often out of personal supplies or food before the end of the month.

I took my roommates to the bathroom and showed them the paper cup with dish soap for shampoo and another paper cup with baking soda for toothpaste. They got quiet real fast. All I could think was if I saw someone struggling, I would have offered them my resources until they could get help. I just didn't understand these roommates.

My roommates decided to prank me by emptying my hair spritz bottle and replace it with water. I just finished taking the hot rollers out of my shoulder-length, blond hair, spritzing it for that '80s hairstyle I was so proud of when all of a sudden my hair went flat. I missed my class so I could stay home and start over. I couldn't afford to replace the spritz for another two weeks. Oh, I wanted to pay them back. My mind went over the devious details, like putting bleach in their spritz bottles, but like usual, I was spineless, non-confrontational, and just absorbed the frustration.

One night, Sheri had come to town to hang out with me. We went to bed around 10:00 p.m. because we were going somewhere early the next morning. My roommates came in around midnight and decided to start laughing loudly, banging cupboards, and breaking out into whispers about what to do next to wake us up. I slept through it all, but my cousin didn't.

The next morning, Sheri and I woke up around six in the morning. Sheri was still mad about what happened the night before. She went into the kitchen area and started slamming cupboards, yelling at the top of her lungs, "Shelly, what do you want for breakfast?"

Then she would pull the pots out and bang on them with a large spoon all the while yelling, "What? I can't hear you, Shelly. What did you say?"

I was dying in my bedroom laughing. I knew she was paying them back. Finally, she slammed the front door three times very hard. This time, two of the roommates got up and said, "We're sorry. We deserve this. You can stop now."

I would forgive them, but I wasn't interested in being their friend either. In my world, they were immature and lacked compassion. I had no need for them. They couldn't see past their own life experiences to allow others to be on a different path. Needless to say, none of them came back the next year; college was too difficult for them. Unfortunately for me, I had to endure constant gossips and shenanigans before they quit.

On Christmas break, I transferred to another room. It was smooth sailing with new roommates after what I had just endured.

I had a few boyfriends while going to college, but nothing lasted over a few weeks. No matter how much I tried, I just couldn't find it in me to fall in love again. There was still nothing inside of me.

During college, I sometimes would sleep in my car and find a gas station or truck stop to clean up. It was only a few days, once in a while, just until I could get back into the dorms.

It did frighten me to sleep in the car. I would wake up several times because I worried that someone would try to get into the car while I was in it. Sometimes it was cold when the weather was snowy, and most of the time I needed to leave the window rolled down about an inch for air.

I just prayed I could wake up if someone was trying to break in. My legs would cramp up because the backseat was small, but once I was asleep, I didn't care.

The part that bugged me the most when sleeping in my car was that I would imagine my dad curled up sleeping in his truck when he took his life. I would lay there and imagine myself in the same situation. I would image myself kicking out the window at the last minute.

Why? Why didn't he kick out the window? Even if his wife didn't love him, he had five kids who needed him. I would get mad all over again. *How come he didn't kick the window out? How come he didn't feel that love for his children break through and change his mind at the last minute?*

I would realize years later that when people are in the mind-set of suicide, they are determined to release themselves from pain that won't go away. Sometimes it is despair that encircles them, and thinking about loved ones doesn't stop them from seeking relief. They think of suicide as a release, and they think others will be relieved to have them out of the way. It is as if they are not in their conscious mind; they are in an alternate sphere that pulls them in and justifies their acts when under normal conditions they would retract from it or be repulsed by it.

I would vow to myself to never put my children through this in the future. I would remember the pain and suffering and let that stop me from inflicting it onto others. This would save me many times as I unknowingly was about to enter many years of off-and-on depression.

I would find myself wanting to run to the outer limits of despair as I had more pain and sadness than I could handle. I just wanted relief.

I graduated from Snow College after two years and transferred to Utah State University to finish a four-year degree. I made sure I earned a secretarial science certificate in addition to an associate's degree at Snow so if I didn't make it through the last two years, I would have a skill to be employable. Once again, I was at Snow College graduation all by myself. The loneliness was becoming a pattern, and I was starting to accept it. The feeling of accomplishment was exuberant! I was beginning to believe that I could make something out of my life. Although my supporters were few, nothing was going to stop me from finishing what I started. I was halfway there! I did eventually graduate with a bachelor's degree in business education with a teaching certificate from USU.

Many times, I was tempted to look for work and not go back to school because it was hard to stay in school, but once I got past the first two years, I became more determined than ever to finish.

Looking back, it was a good thing for me not to have a serious relationship or to get married like many of my roommates, or I would have never finished four years of college. Life didn't get easier; it got harder! I recognized there was a small window for me to bear down and get a degree without the demands of a family. If I miss that window, the task would become nearly impossible.

The important thing for me at the time was to remember during this time was that I wasn't alone. I had to develop faith that God was opening doors for me and helping me to remain safe, not just physically but spiritually and emotionally. I needed this time in my life to accomplish certain things that would be beneficial to change the course of my life later.

Of course, when you are a teenager, that is hard to see; it took my growing older and looking back on the situation to appreciate what was really happening. Thank goodness I kept journals so I could measure my progress. All the tears and disappointments were actually necessary to bring about a greater blessing.

Unfortunately for Kristen and Terry, coming into their teen years the nightmare was just getting started. Scott was not with them anymore; he was on his own now. He lived with different girlfriends and complete strangers off and on. He started to settle down by marrying Jozette and eventually had five children with her. By now, he was drinking heavily, doing hard drugs, acting out violently, and putting his family on a roller coaster of events that eventually ended his marriage. Scott would also start his long history of being in and out of incarceration.

Kristen and Terry ran away from home and lived with different friends as "spendovers" for three days at a time so other parents wouldn't catch on they were runaways.

Eventually, they were caught and sent back to Mom. Neither of them started high school, and both spent time in juvenile hall.

Kristen was introduced to Carson's friends as a date at the age of thirteen. I remember seeing her by surprise on a visit to Gila Bend, and she had bleached her hair and wore heavy makeup and a cropped shirt. I was horrified. All I could think was, *This would not have been acceptable when I was a teen. What has happened to my baby sister?* I questioned her about her clothing, and she was offended that I was being judgmental and didn't understand my disappointment at all. She liked how she was dressed!

My mom still wouldn't leave Carson, who was an alcoholic and regularly beat her over the years. I offered her several times to come live with me as an adult, but she refused every time. I couldn't figure out why Mom didn't want to leave that environment. I thought she would be embarrassed, but she was only fearful that I would have Kristen and Terry taken away. It was hard for me to accept this was her answer, but she insisted she was okay, it was her choice, and I need not worry about her. As pointed out in the book about sociopathic people, as long as she was having a good time, that was all that mattered; people with psychosis are only interested in their own needs.

Kristen would become pregnant at fifteen with her first of seven children.

A SEASON OF LOVE

I was faithful at keeping a journal through college. I had learned early on that it was therapy for me to write. It would also be the connection for me when I figured out who my husband was going to be and how I could trust love again.

It was January 1982, Logan, Utah. I was in my junior year of college at Utah State University. I had a dream in which I was visiting my grandmother in her shanty in Arizona. We were laughing and talking. She was puttering around with something in the kitchen, and I was in front of the mirror getting ready for a date.

I was nervous but excited. I was almost done with my makeup when I got the feeling that whoever was coming to the door to pick me up was the one I was supposed to marry. I asked Grandma, "Is that true, that's who I am supposed to marry?"

She said, "Yes."

Just then, the doorbell buzzed, and I got too nervous and couldn't go to the door. She said, "Answer the door, honey, and don't be afraid to love him."

Then Grandma disappeared. I went to open the door, and there was this bright light at the door, and all I could see was a shadow of a man standing there. Then I woke up.

No! I wanted to see who it was! I tried to go back to sleep and see who it was, but it was too late. I was so disappointed. I didn't get to see "him," and Grandma was gone! Oh, I wanted that dream to keep going.

I wrote about it in my journal. Those dreams where Grandma visited me are so vivid and seem so real. I can't stop thinking about them for days.

Two months before this dream, I was dating Ken Kennedy, one of my neighbors. It was more like a television buddy who would come over to watch the sitcom *M*A*S*H* after the nightly news.

Ken invited me to go home with him for Christmas knowing I didn't have any place to go. These "pity" invites had never worked out before, and this one wouldn't either. He didn't want to give his family the impression he had a girlfriend, but he didn't want me to stop cuddling with him either when we got back.

When we got back from the break, I put an end to that right away. I got my answer that he wasn't interested in me long term. It was okay; I just needed to keep looking. What was odd was that my next-door neighbor Lynette Morel, with whom I was pretty good friends with, didn't hesitate to start hitting on Ken and go with him on a date or two. Maybe they were just TV buddies too.

Our church singles group was having night skiing at the local resort. I asked Lynette if she wanted to drive up with me. She emphatically said, "No, my new boyfriend, Reed, is there, and he and his buddies are having a guys' night out. I don't want him to think I am following him."

I was a little taken aback that she thought it was appropriate for a boyfriend to tell her to stay away from something, but whatever, it was her boyfriend. I pushed back, "Lynette, you are not going to be with Reed. You are going to be with me. I promise we won't bother Reed and his friends."

She agreed to go with me. We headed off up the canyon for about a twenty-minute drive. The minute we pulled into the parking lot, a skier was heading straight for my car as the parking lot edges up against the bottom of the slope.

I was mesmerized by this good-looking guy who was skiing toward me. *Wow! How come I don't meet guys like this one?* He was tall, with dark hair and cute little mustache. I just wanted to stare.

Just then Lynette interrupted, "Shelly, there's Reed! Now what do I do?" She was pointing to the guy I was staring at!

I assured her she was okay, just follow me. Reed skied right up to us and said, "Hello, Lynette. I thought I told you this was guys' night out. What are you doing here?"

Oh my, what a jerk! All I could think was, *Walk away, Lynette!* I interrupted, "She's with me. We are here for the single's activity." Then I turned and started to walk away.

Lynette lowered her voice and was talking to Reed about something when she said, "Shelly, go on up to the lodge, I'm going to stay with Reed for a little bit, I'll see you later."

Well, well, well. Looks can be deceiving. How could I fall for someone so arrogant? At least I didn't have to hang around with those two. In my mind, he was a jerk, and Lynette was too accommodating! I headed up to the lodge and enjoyed the hot chocolate and dancing.

Toward the end of the evening, Lynette came over to tell me Reed was taking her home, but he wanted to know if I was interested in going on a double date with him and his friend Brooke.

I was stunned for a minute. Blind dates never work out, but how do I say no without hurting her feelings? She was, however, a good friend and my next-door neighbor.

"Sure, why not," I said. "When do you guys want to go?" I asked.

"In two days, Wednesday night, he wants to go to the movies," Lynette rattled it off and then gave me the miniature wave as she was rushing back to him.

Well, Wednesday came, and Reed showed up with Brooke in his dark-gray 1968 restored Firebird. What a coincidence, I had a restored Firebird at one time!

I got into the backseat with Brooke, and my heart sank. This guy was a freshman! It was like I was dating a younger brother! *Ughhhhh!* This date had better go quickly.

Reed was playing a Bob Seger song in his eight-track player. That was a pleasant surprise. Bob Seger was one of my favorites too. I don't know what started it, but once Reed got to talking, I couldn't help myself to spar with him and let him know he wasn't as cool as he thought he was. It seems like I was still a little miffed from the first time I met him.

By the end of the evening, Reed and I were talking like old lost friends getting acquainted again. We had so much in common it was eerie.

We both had a Firebird, we listened to the same music, we both played sports in high school, we both were business majors, we both were competitive, and we had the same sense of humor. I had never met anyone who was so much like me.

There was this one moment at the end of the evening when we were both one-upping each other, and he stopped midsentence as we realized we were not together. We were with other people. We needed to leave our little bubble of conversation and attraction and include the other two.

Reed and his '68 Firebird car (left). Shelly and Reed after a church function in Clifton, Idaho (1982).

I didn't think much more about Reed after that night as he was the boyfriend of a good friend. I just didn't think he was a jerk anymore.

About a week later, I went to an all-day water-park activity and was physically drained by the sun. My hair was dried back away from my face, and I had no makeup on after swimming. I was pink from being in the sun for the first time this year, and I didn't want to shower until I got home and could take a long nap. I crashed on the couch when I walked into my apartment and went right to sleep.

A few hours later, there was a knock on the door. I could barely wake up. I thought I would ignore it, but the knock came again. I stumbled my way over to the door. Just as I opened it, the sun was setting, and all I could see was this bright light in my eyes from a the setting sun and the shadow of a man standing there. I asked, "Whoever you are, can you move over here so I can see you?"

Just as my eyes focused, I saw that it was Reed.

I could have died at that moment. I didn't think he was there for me, but for history's sake, I'm glad I answered the door. He had a look of hesitation on his face but mustered up the courage to finish why he was there.

"Reed, what are you doing here? Lynette lives next door," I said as I rubbed my fingers through my dry, crackling hair. I looked hammered. What's worse was Reed had no idea of what I had been doing.

"I'm not looking for Lynette. I'm looking for you," Reed said.

"Oh no, I can't do this, Lynette is my friend, I won't do this," I said with fear in my voice.

"No worries, Shelly, Lynette and I broke up last week. It's okay," Reed said. He didn't assure me at all.

"I can't. I just can't. Lynette is my friend. I can't go out with her ex-boyfriend," I repeated. Just then, it came to me. Lynette went out with Ken right after I broke up with him. There is no code of honor to break with her.

"Okay, I will go. I just remembered she went out with one of my ex-boyfriends," I said. I was still very nervous. I just wasn't sure this was going to be worth the gossip from the girls in my apartment.

"Great, can I pick you up Wednesday at seven? We are going up the canyon for a cookout with my friend Doug and his new wife, Connie," he said. He didn't stick around; he probably sensed how uncomfortable I was feeling with my hair sticking up, no makeup, and my tired, sunburned face.

Well, Wednesday came. Seven o'clock came, seven fifteen came, seven thirty came, seven forty-five came, and now I was mad. *Did he stand me up? Was he having second thoughts? Was he not honorable enough to call and cancel?*

I frantically searched for my keys. I wasn't going to stay home. I wasn't going to give him the satisfaction of being here should he try to show up later. *How could he be so rude?*

I turned to lock the key to my apartment and skipped up the steps, when there he was coming down the steps. He was in a good mood. "Hello! You ready?" he said.

What? He didn't even have a clue how late he was nor did he apologize for being late. He just put his arm underneath mine and escorted me to his car.

Okay, should I be mad at him? Should I ask him why he was late? Should I just forgive him and just move forward with the evening? You know me, no spine. I didn't say a word. He carried on with his conversation and was excited to get the evening started.

We laid out the salads and started a fire pit for the steaks. Doug and Connie were congenial, but had no interest whatsoever in talking; they couldn't keep their hands off each other. I was so annoyed every time I was around them that I would jump up and grab the Frisbee and start playing over in another area trying to get Reed's attention and staying away from Doug and Connie.

As soon as we ate, Doug and Connie excused themselves and headed out. Now it was just Reed and I.

Things started to change quickly. Reed invited me to sit by him near the fire to talk. It was the strangest feeling in the world. It was as if I had known him from somewhere. I was so excited to hear him talk and anxious to hear what he had to say next.

The fire was crackling, and suddenly Reed jumped up. There was a rustling noise in the bush next to him. He sat down on the other side of me. I just grinned. For starters, the noise wasn't enough to scare me, but he didn't even notice he was using me to shield him from any possible danger!

That night was magical. The air seemed thicker, and time seemed to slow down. Everything was calm and exciting at the same time. We talked until three in the morning, watching the fire burn. Before we knew it, it was time to go home. We didn't want to leave, but we had to. We had classes the next day.

He walked me to the door of my apartment. Just as I turned around to say good night, he placed his hand under my chin and gave me a gentle kiss on the lips.

"I've enjoyed the evening immensely," he whispered.

"Me too."

"Can I see you tomorrow?"

"Sure, what time?" I whispered back.

"Around five," he said as he walked away back to his car.

I'm not sure if I could trust my feelings again. I wrote about him in my journal and called it a night. How do you tell someone you just met that you have fallen in love with them? That's how I was feeling for the first time in three years. I was feeling love again.

Things moved quickly; after six weeks, school ended, and summer was upon us. Reed proposed in July, and we were married on September 11, 1982. I often joke I should have noticed the date was 9/11. Years later, we would share this date with infamy.

It would be the most important decision I would ever make—to marry Reed. God knew who I needed. He left a clue in a dream with my grandmother as the messenger. It was about a month after we started dating that I made the connection in my journal, about my dream and what happened the first time he asked me out. If I ever doubted throughout the years whether I married the right person, I need only to look at my journal. God picked him out for me.

However, it wasn't a seamless transition; I soon discovered I had trust issues that I could not control. I noticed I couldn't trust anything that required someone else to be in control of me. For instance, something as simple as someone else driving a car would strike fear through me. To this day, I can't be the one who teaches our teenagers how to drive. Another example would be trusting Reed to provide for us financially. I constantly felt the need to be looking for new ways to make money so that I have some control in the matter.

Another trust issue is one of personal touch. For whatever reason, I cannot have someone touch my face, especially around my ears. It is as if there are a thousand ants crawling on me. Reed understands this, and we do what we need to so that I won't go into withdrawals.

However, when I had babies or toddlers, I could hardly put them down. I had no issues with sleeping next to them or having them hang on me all day if they wanted. When I had teenagers, it became more and more difficult for me to be cuddly with them. Reed gladly filled in that spot as he is a cuddly person.

On more than one occasion, I would wake up in the morning after we all fell asleep watching a movie, and there would be Reed and several children draped across him on his side of the bed and me with the other half of the bed. Everyone just knew Mom wasn't the "cuddler" and Dad was.

As long as we talked about it as a family and everyone knew my limitations, we were fine. I have a daughter who will kiss the top of my head and tells me she loves me rather than risk an awkward wimpy hug. I have a daughter who likes to give me side hugs (one arm hugs) so I don't tense up. My kids are beautiful. They understand me. They tell me they love me with every phone call. It is not hard for them to express intimacy freely although I still struggle.

Reed is valiant and determined to live life by the rules. He is intensely loyal to a fault. Given that I needed to overcome some personal issues with trust, this was a redeeming quality in him. Reed is a wizard with money. He knows how to save, invest, and save some more even when there is very little money to go around. He is a smart, educated, and stable. He is almost immovable once he makes up his mind about something. He takes very little risk and considers himself "the tortoise" in the fable *The Tortoise and the Hare*, going slowly and steadily but winning the race. Because of his great inner strength, I never worry about him putting our future at risk. I would often get mad at him because I wanted to take some risks with starting different business ventures, but he always has the inner strength to hold back and not succumb to the enticement money offers.

I don't have to worry that he will get mad at me or abandon me. He is solid, and God knew what would calm my heart and give me an anchor for life.

Reed and I graduated together from college; I went on to teach while he went on to get a master's of business administration degree.

With my degree, I was able to teach high school for a few years at West Side High School in Dayton, Idaho; and then do substituting once I needed to stay home more. Later in life, I would start a business that required me to understand accounting, marketing, and office procedures to be successful. The business would become the fulcrum point of our change in wealth and control over our financial future.

Teaching high school and postsecondary college for two years was fulfilling and allowed me to work with teenagers. I tried to elevate their lives in a way that would make a difference. I sensed their fragile nature and vulnerability for making decisions at their age and put a strong emphasis on helping them go through college and to believe in themselves.

While teaching high school, I wanted to do the same scholarship award that was given to me when I was in high school. I received a small scholarship from the Lions Club when I graduated from high school, which inspired me to go to college. I sent a letter to all the surrounding businesses in the valley asking for donations to a high school scholarship fund. I collected over three thousand dollars. I divided the money up to how many seniors as I had in my advance classes.

I tried to make learning fun. I wanted to build relationships with these students to inspire them to move out of their comfort zone and do great things. Most of my students were from an agriculture community that had been farming for generations and college was almost unheard of. It was heartwarming to learn years later that most of the students I pushed into college actually finished college!

This was also the introduction of computers to the school. Our school district had zero computers. No one knew how to use them or what to use them for. I contacted the State Vocational Education Department and asked them what I could do to get a computer or two in my classroom. They said that whatever funds I could raise they would match it. Perfect, now I knew where to start.

I got the local Lions Club to donate eight hundred dollars. I got other valley businesses to donate also. We had small fund-raisers with the students. In the end, we had two thousand dollars. The state matched that and now we had four thousand dollars. Back then, computers were very expensive and had a small capacity for storage. Computers used large floppy disks and most had an industrial-metal look to them. Apple was just coming out with personal computers that were made from hard plastic. I could get two Kaypro brand computers with a printer for the price of one Apple computer at the education rate. I ended up with four Kaypro computers total.

I taught night classes to the local farmers on how to set up database programs, most specifically dBASE II, to keep inventory and how to use WordStar for word processing. I would teach them how to build a spreadsheet on Lotus 1-2-3 for simple calculations. Many needed basic typewriting skills first. I was thrilled to see them coming into the future of business with computers.

I taught accounting, shorthand, typing and computers. I was also the cheerleading and the basketball coach. I wanted to give back; I wanted to share my talents to help others attain gratification from achievement. It felt good to give back. It felt good to know my life wasn't wasted, that I was important to someone else. My losses in life didn't seem so big once I got involved in inspiring others.

Once Reed finished his MBA degree, we moved to Sacramento, California, for his first job as an auditor for the California State legislature.

PARALLEL LIVES

Reed and I moved our tiny family of two children to Sacramento, California, for his first job with the auditor-general's office. It was the first time either of us had lived in California and we had no relatives or friends near us. We found an apartment in one of the suburbs known as the Pocket area as it was a housing track that bordered the winding Sacramento River and formed a pocket.

Our new life was promising, and we were excited to continue building our future by saving for a home and climbing the career ladder. It became apparent quickly that one income in California was barely going to cover the rent and our basic necessities, and that was with a college degree! Reed and I made the decision that I should find a part-time teaching job to save money for a down payment on a home and then I would quit to stay home full-time with the children.

I secured a job with Western Career College as a computer instructor and a medical assistant teacher for three hours a day. It was perfect because I didn't want to be away full-time with my two little ones not in school yet. I was thrilled to be working with post–high school students encouraging them to get an education and making life easier by having a degree and feeling content that we could buy a home in a few years.

This was the early '80s, and women were leaving home in record numbers to work. The economy was booming; however, it required nearly two incomes to qualify for a home loan. After all I had been through as a child, I was determined to stay home with my children if ever I was going to have them. I really struggled with this decision and was at peace as long as there was a distinct goal and end date for me to return home.

A few months after arriving in Sacramento, I got pregnant. This was baby number 3, and my last baby was about four months old. We'd always like to say, "How did that happen?" when I would get pregnant as if that would take the responsibility off of us. "It's okay," we'd tell ourselves. "We always wanted a large family." In California, having three children was bordering a huge family. This baby taught us that it was tough to carry three kids when you only had two sets of arms. This one felt like we were having twins since both were in diapers and needed to be carried. Once Danielle was born, I put in my notice at work. We were almost to our payment goal for a home, and the school took over five months to find my replacement. The school thought I would change my mind at any time because I loved it there, and they loved having me there, but I knew I could come back years later to teach, but I couldn't have back those years that my children were babies and toddlers.

I enjoyed being a mother. It was an eye-opener to me how much I loved my children. I would go to the ends of the earth for them. I could never imagine hitting them or belittling them. I could never imagine asking them to find another place to live when they became teenagers.

I couldn't imagine cutting them off emotionally. I never would know how my mother felt so comfortable doing those things, but it didn't stop me from thinking about her decisions.

As I would dress my children for school, I would think of the times I went to school in clothes that didn't fit, weren't my gender, or weren't my size. Yet that was how I went to school. I had a neighbor when I was nine who asked me once, "Who dresses you in the morning?" while I was walking home from school. I looked down and saw what I was wearing, and she was right. I had on a boy's shirt with a dress slip sticking out of my jeans. I looked away and walked off quickly so I could get home and change.

When my children were misbehaving, I couldn't imagine pulling out a belt and hitting these innocent, tender souls! Instead, I had an immense urge to pick them up, ask them why they were doing something wrong, and then tell them with kisses to their cheeks how much I loved them for changing their behavior to good behavior.

Several years later, hearts would break when news came to us that Kristen was on her fifth child and still unable to care for them. She had problems with alcohol and drugs, and it impaired her ability to care for her children.

Kristen had an anger problem. She severely beat one of her boys who was four years old. We tried to get her to let us adopt TJ, but she changed her mind at the last minute. We did get her to let Mechelle come stay with us for awhile but Mechelle would return home and resume her responsibilities as the second mother caring for five other siblings.

One night, when Mechelle was fourteen, Kristen called her from a bar to come pick her up as she was too drunk to drive herself home. Mechelle loaded up her siblings and drove to the bar. On the way home, Mechelle rolled the car off of a ravine. Everyone in the car ejected. The eight-month-old baby was still in the car seat, but suffered a broken leg. A four-year old suffered a broken shoulder. Mechelle would die of a broken neck.

The funeral for Mechelle was traumatic. Kristen was under the influence of drugs, and her emotions ranged from hysterical to angry. Kristen did not sit with any of her children. The children were dispersed throughout the chapel, sitting with friends or alone. I was confused by the family dynamics, but I wanted to be a supportive bystander and helpful during a time like this, so I did what I could to console the younger siblings as I found them. However, Kristen did not want me at the funeral. She never said why; she just ignored me and refused to talk to me. At one time, she walked up to me and, without saying a word, tried to slap me in the face. I grabbed her hand before she could hit me. She pulled away and walked off.

I spent two days driving to get there and two days back, and I was regretting that I even worried about her. I visited my mom after the funeral asking why Kristen was angry at me, but she was tight-lipped about Kristen and her circumstances.

Kristen had two suicide attempts: once before Mechelle's death and once after. Her attempts were mostly threats and led to more counseling. A few years later, Kristen was partying at an apartment in Denver with her boyfriend. An estranged girlfriend showed up with a shotgun, and the police were alerted. The police surrounded the apartment and raided, apprehending the girlfriend. Kristen, however, would lose her children permanently because of the drugs that were found in her house, and she had multiple probation violations.

Three of the boys returned to their biological father. Another son, Michael, from another father went into foster care and then later adopted out. Kristen and her children were granted visitation with Michael for a few years and eventually no more visits.

Kristen would return to Kansas to live with my mother, enter rehab for her alcohol and drug addictions, and eventually find another boyfriend and have two more children, Glen and Jacob. She was in a holding pattern for now.

Terry had married at the age of sixteen to Astrud, who was also sixteen. They had three children. Terry would become severely depressed and was diagnosed with schizophrenia early in his adult life. He was addicted to drugs and alcohol and could not hold down a job for more than a week in his entire life. His wife and three children would ride a roller coaster of emotions with him not fully aware of what was wrong with him.

There came a time when Terry's wife had to put a restraining order against him, divorced him, and moved out with their three children. Terry would continually resurface and create chaos for them wherever they moved to. Terry had two suicide attempts during this time of his life and was hospitalized for each one.

Scott was incarcerated most of these years on burglary, theft, violence, alcohol, and drug-related offenses. His wife would divorce him and move on to rebuild her life.

Having children was a season of healing for me. I could give love unconditionally. I could feel love with those little arms wrapped around my neck hugging me. I could be important to someone. I could make a difference in their happiness levels. I could be the boss and that meant I could pardon them from all of life's burdens and spoil them with love and attention. I had a new life. It wasn't filled with money or lacking disappointment, but it was an awesome life. It was my new world.

I was mindful that my first child was a girl, and I did not want to make her the live-in maid, Cinderella, or the second wife as I had been, being the oldest girl in a large family. I would generally ask her if she could help; I usually paid her in extra privileges or money. This daughter had never told me no, nor had she been disrespectful toward me even in her teen years. She was the *perfect* firstborn. She was a leader with her siblings and yet was kind toward them at the same time.

I became determined to shield my children from my past. I had very little interaction with my mother and siblings at this point. I didn't want to burden my children with sorrow for past events because I know that when you expose children to dysfunction, suicide, or abuse, they tend to absorb those feelings, and it usually becomes a part of their thought processes.

My mother would visit me twice in twenty years. In one of her earlier visits, the conversation stayed cordial, but it was obvious that we were no longer mother and daughter; we were more like old friends.

She took no interest in my children as a grandmother, and she never could quite bring herself to mother me. I had to explain to the kids when Grandma came to visit why she wasn't like Grandma McDermott. My mother didn't allow the kids to sit on her lap. She didn't want to watch movies with them or even engage in conversation much. My mom kept with her mantra that I grew up with: "Kids are to be seen and not heard." Since she rarely visited, as a consequence, the kids weren't much interested in her either.

Once when she came to visit, she was telling me a story about how she and Carson met *after* Dad died, and immediately I could tell it had been rehearsed, including all the important requirements of how he rescued her from a disastrous situation; however, it was all a lie. It was the story she had been telling all her friends and grandchildren.

Did she forget I lived through those days too? Did she forget I would remember that she ran off with Carson? She would tell a story of meeting him after my father died, and he was kind enough to help her put her life together and raise her five children. *Did she forget that she put me, Jerry, and Scott to the curb like garbage?*

It finally came to me that she was mentally sick. She was good at manipulating others to feel sorry for her and to draw a narrative that made her and Carson out to be victims and heroes at the same time.

We were sitting at a restaurant, and I finally said, "Mom, I lived through this, and this is not how it happened!" For the first time, I was irritated with her and showed some disdain toward her.

She stopped for a minute and looked at me, kind of, puzzled and said, "I guess we all have a different memory of what happened." That was when I realized we couldn't rebuild our relationship because she wasn't living in reality.

I pushed away my contempt. I knew that it was my responsibility to love her despite all that had happened. I didn't have to trust her, but it was my responsibility to treat her as any other human with disabilities. For some odd reason, I was overcome with compassion for her.

I would even go further and honor her as my mother for giving me birth. That took some practice, but that was my decision to do so, and I did.

Although I recognized this deficiency in her early on, I always let it trip me up after each visit whether in person or on the phone. I would mourn her leaving and wish I had a real mother. Even as a young mother, I still needed to be mothered.

I would see mothers and daughters in stores shopping together, and it would tug at my heart and bring tears to my eyes. When my friends would have babies, their mothers would dote over them and bring them baby items. I would be brokenhearted as mine was alive but absent. I would do crochet or sew baby quilts for each child as a memorial of their birth; I am not going to follow my mother's lack of traditions.

After my third child, doctors told me that I had endometriosis, and I would not be able to have more children. I was upset because I wanted to make that decision on my own, not have nature tell me that! So, I became determined to get pregnant anyhow, and as luck would have it, I had no problem. Welcome, baby number 4—another beautiful daughter, Brittany Nichole.

While I was nine months pregnant with this baby, I needed to stop at the store for a quick run to buy a gift card for a baby shower I was going to later for a friend. If this wasn't enough to stop me from having more children, I don't know what could have. I really felt as if I could see, for the first time, how my parents might have been so quick to yell and scream at us kids. I very seldom went to the store with more than one child as I learned early on that even one child could turn the whole trip into a disaster. I would wait to go to the store until Reed came home to avoid taking the children, but this trip was going to be short; I could manage it.

I felt particularly confident on this trip that if we went in quickly and came out quickly, there would be very little time for something disastrous to happen. I gave each of my three children their instructions. Katryna, who was eight, wanted to know if they could have a candy bar at checkout if they were good. I told her yes and she could go straight to the candy section and start picking it out, that I would meet her there. I told Lucas, who was four, to come with me and hold my hand. I told Danielle, who was three, to hold Mom's other hand and help me walk to the card aisle.

Well, upon entering, Katryna went straight for the candy. Danielle broke from my hand and ran toward the carts. I yelled at her to come back, that Mommy didn't need a cart this time. I could barely walk much less run with my big belly. Lucas, sensing that I needed a hero to retrieve my daughter, decided to run after her. Upon seeing him, Danielle squealed with delight, and the chase was on.

Danielle decided to push the cart as she was running. She ran her cart right into another cart and bounced back just a little. The snarly lady with reading glasses looked over just long enough to show her disgust. That didn't stop Danielle; she looked back at Lucas and decided she still had time to run a little harder. She ran her cart into another shopper's cart just as Lucas was tackling her.

Danielle was screaming, I was waddling quickly, and Lucas was getting scared. He wasn't sure if I was going to be too happy, so he jumped up and grabbed my leg and buried his head on my thigh. I grabbed Danielle who was screaming wildly and threw her over my shoulder while she was kicking her legs back and forth trying to get down. There were about ten people standing at various places around me who completely stopped in their shopping to watch this spectacle.

Danielle wouldn't stop screaming or kicking my belly, and I couldn't get Lucas to let go of my leg. I just started dragging him to the door hanging on. I wanted to spank Danielle because she still had not stopped with the screaming and kicking my belly, but there were too many people watching, and I just needed to get out quickly.

Just then, Katryna showed up with a candy bar in her hand. She held it up to her nose and, happy with excitement, exclaimed, "I found the one I want, Mommy!"

I hated to tell her, but I said, "Not now, we can't, Mommy needs to go to the car."

Without a breath, Katryna let out a loud screaming grunt, "But you promised, you promised!"

Dragging two of the kids with my big belly, one of them still screaming, I finally made it out to the van. I slung the door open, pried Danielle off my shoulder, and tossed her into the car seat. I pulled Lucas off next and tossed him into his seat. I pointed to Katryna to get in the car with my finger. I looked up just in time to see the people standing at the door who had followed me to watch the event's finale. I couldn't lose it now. I wouldn't give them the pleasure of seeing me become a crazy, mad mommy. I got in the van and drove off.

Of course, I scolded Danielle, thanked Lucas, consoled Katryna, and secretly vowed never to take them all at once to the store again! Then I patted myself on the back for overcoming a family history of hitting and yelling when under stress.

We made friends with another family down the street who had six children. Our kids matched up in ages, and it was enjoyable to have friends who understood our large family ways. We spent a lot of time together, and it seemed as though we could have had ten children each, and our lives would not be much different. We were about family. We were about raising them to be strong in faith. We saw each child as a blessing and a gift. We never questioned if we had done the wrong thing having large families.

Well, baby number 5 came, and once again, we were surprised and wanted to know "how did that happen?" Another girl. We were not in the planning phase, but we never saw a baby as anything but the grandest experience in life. I knew then that birth control didn't work for me. I needed to find a more permanent method if I did not want to have more children. Once again, I took it up with God.

I knew then that after every baby is born, you are so in love with that new family member, you could consider twelve more! Then when the child turns two, you wonder how you had more than two! So, I would start my prayers to God asking if I should stop having children or does he have another plan for me. Society was telling me I passed my limit, yet I wanted to get God's input too.

When Hannah was five months old, I was sitting under a tree reading a book at the lake with her next to me. I put the book down to run to the van for a diaper.

As I got to the van, a whirlwind came around me, and I heard a voice as distinct as two people talking. It said to me, "Mommy, there's not just one more of us. There are two."

I stopped immediately. *Did I just hear what I heard?* Then I started to cry. Just then Reed saw me and came over to hug me and asked what was wrong. I told him what just happened.

He hugged me again and said, "That's okay, honey, you don't have to have them both at the same time." He was trying to console me, but it had the opposite effect; after being pregnant five times before, I would love to have them both at the same time to kill two birds with one stone!

I knew what I heard. I knew that God knew what I had just heard. I didn't question it anymore. I went forward and had two more children.

Because my sixth child, Mikayla Marie, was our fifth girl, I really wanted to have a boy, if at all possible, for our last one. But if not, we were always ready for more girls.

Just before my seventh child was born, I had another dream. This time I saw my father standing in a field with wheat or tall grass swaying; I was gazing at his eyes and was a little curious as to why he was standing there. I kept staring at his face. I knew who he was, and I felt like he was beckoning me. He had a slight grin, and he held out his hand to me. I was so busy looking at him that I almost didn't notice he was holding the hand of a small child about the age of four, a little boy with very red hair. Then I woke up.

A few days later, Reed and I went for an ultrasound. The technician asked me if we wanted to know the sex of the baby. I looked at Reed and said, "Sure, but I already know what it is."

She asked me what I thought it was. I said, "A boy."

She said, "You're right!"

My eyes started to tear up. I knew it was another message from God that I had done the right thing. Yes, this boy grew up and had very red hair. Cody was also born on my birthday; another secret wish I had when I was younger was fulfilled.

It wasn't enough for me just to have children and put them on a shelf until they grow up and move out or to be seen and not heard, I wanted to start some family traditions that were ours. I wanted my children to look back on their childhood and say, I did this and that with my parents, and that's how I want to raise my children.

We decided early on to take the children on dates individually to give them some one-on-one time. It was just to go get an ice cream, but it was an incredible feeling in the car as if the whole world revolved around just the two of you for a few minutes.

We started with a family council and game night together once a week. We would use this time to bring up what we saw as needing improvement and opened it up as a topic for discussion. What was amazing was how effective this technique was in getting children to find solutions for their own problems. They owned the responsibility of it. This actually worked for several behavior issues, and I rarely had to raise my voice, and I never had to spank them.

Another tradition was we would meet up with Dad every Friday downtown on his lunchtime and go to the nearest park close to his office. This particular park had a small lake and ducks. We would have a small sandwich for lunch and feed ducks. No matter how many times we did that, it never got old. We felt like we were rescuing Daddy from a hard day's work and fortifying him with more energy to go back and "slay the evil dragons at work." This endeared the children to their father. They learned to appreciate his labor for them and give them an image to connect to where Daddy went during the day when he was working for them.

In return, Dad would make the children "awful waffles" on the weekends because they were "awfully good" to reciprocate his love.

On one of those trips downtown to pick up Reed for lunch, we would see the normal occurrence of panhandlers at every traffic light with cardboard signs asking for money. One time my son asked me, "Mom, what can we do about that?"

I told him, "Nothing today, but from now on when we go downtown, we would put in our trunk shoeboxes with canned soup, crackers, and drinks. When we see someone who is needy, we give them a shoebox." This spurred us on to an even greater project.

Every year at Christmas, we would each decorate a box, fill it with items such as blankets, shirts, scarves, gloves, candy, drinks, food certificates, hygiene products, etc., and then go a few days before Christmas and randomly hand them out to homeless people we would catch being alone.

Only one of us at a time could get out of the van with our box. We didn't say much, just handed the homeless person a box, wish them a Merry Christmas, and run back to the van. Sometimes it resulted in a handshake or a big smile and a wave from the homeless person. The rule was that the recipient had to be alone as to not draw attention to or embarrass anyone.

We continue this tradition still today, sixteen years later. It is our preparation for the real meaning of Christmas. The first time we went out, we came back around to one of the first streets where we handed a box out, and there was an elderly man who spread the blanket out, put the food out on the blanket as if it were a buffet, and he was on his knees with his hands clasped saying a prayer.

Shiny toys on Christmas morning pale in comparison to the happiness we have witnessed when sharing our resources with homeless people. We were stunned. We were silent. We were humbled. We were ready for Christmas.

It wasn't easy raising seven children on one income in a high-cost-of-living state like California, but everything worked out fine. Frugality was an income. My commitment to my family, and having a large one, was burning deep within me, and I was willing to put it all on the line to work hard and succeed in helping my children have a healthy and happy family life.

I didn't have time any more to worry about the past. I was consumed with little arms hugging me and children telling me they loved me. They truly filled my love tank that had been so empty for so long. I was growing too. Of all the experiences I have had, raising my children has taught me more about myself and stretched me further than any other experiences I have had.

Having my own family, after living in a dysfunctional one growing up, was one of the best ways I could get over the pain and misery of my past. When I thought about the events and circumstances that caused me pain, embarrassment, or shame, then I knew those things were wrong. I became determined not to do those things to my children.

My mother was a screamer, and it caused my body to shiver in fear, and my father was a beater, and it caused me to wear bruises and have low self-esteem; I became determined not to do those things to my children. I also become steadfast in preserving my marriage because I was determined never to put my children through a breakup. I had to find a way to renew my marriage and keep it healthy even when I wanted to be left alone or was feeling neglected.

I thought about the things that made me feel loved and inspired to be a better person. I wanted to be that same inspiration for my children. I wanted to break the cycle and stand as a sentinel for the next generation.

I petitioned the Lord in prayer, kept journals, had a very supportive spouse, and watched other successful mothers intently to learn patterns that would help me to be successful. I didn't care if I was different from the rest of the neighborhood with my large family. I didn't care if people wanted to see me punish my children harshly, and instead, I hugged the child and used a gentle corrective voice. It was my turn to make a difference.

Strangers verbally mocked me on more than one occasion about having so many children. One time, I was at a grocery store buying bread. I used to buy my bread in bulk and then freeze it so I wouldn't have to go to the store every week. One day, a woman standing behind me in line said, "You don't mind if I ask how many people you are buying for, do you?" Of course, I was about seven months' pregnant with my sixth child. I told her I had five other children and a husband. You'd think she saw a snake the way she started screaming. "Six kids! Six kids! You've got to be kidding me! Who has six kids these days?" I just continued to load my groceries onto the conveyor belt refusing to engage in conversation.

She wasn't satisfied with me ignoring her, so she turned to the people behind her and started pointing to me. "This woman has six kids! Can you believe that?" And then to the cashier, she asked, "Can you imagine that? Six kids?"

The voice in my head said, *You never have to apologize* for being a large family. It doesn't matter what size your family is. You never have to be accountable to others for your personal decisions, you just need to be accountable to your children.

THE DEVIL IS ON THE PORCH AGAIN

Kristen would have two more sons, Glen and Jacob. Kristen violated probation with another drug and alcohol incident, and these boys were taken away and put into foster care at ages two and four just as her older children were living in foster care permanently. This was more than Kristen wanted to deal with.

Kristen had drowned herself with alcohol and drugs and drove a convertible car over one hundred miles per hour before rolling it and killing herself by breaking her neck, the same way Mechelle had died. There was no suicide note, but it was very much on our minds that she was tired and had given up.

Her funeral was the first time all of us kids had been together at once since Dad died twenty-four years earlier. Scott was there in an orange prison jumpsuit with chains on his feet. Jerry and Tess were able to make it. It was a bittersweet reunion. I had not seen him since high school. Terry and Astrud drove through the night two states away.

Kristen's three sons who were in foster care stole a car in Farmington, New Mexico, determined to make it their mother's funeral. Glen and Jacob were allowed to attend the funeral, but that would be the last time any of us would be allowed to see them as they were adopted out. Reed and I tried to adopt them, but the caseworker was angry with my mother and Kristen and recommended to the judge that the children sever ties with the family.

I was having a hard time shedding any tears for Kristen. I was angry with her as I saw her children being neglected and subjected to abuse. I knew the children didn't know any better. It reminded me of my own childhood. It was hard for me to reconcile that a mother could be so detrimental to her own children like that and continue the pattern of abuse with seven children. Her funeral was small and intimate. There were not many people who knew her. Once again, my mother was being less than honest about the details of Kristen and her problems. How can any of us help if we are kept in the dark? These young children could have been spared from pain and abuse if my mom would have let others know about the conditions.

A few years later, Terry ended up homeless in Salt Lake City, Utah, and addicted to meth. It happened to be the year that we made a major move from California, after twenty-three years, to a small town on the back of the Wasatch Mountains in Morgan, Utah.

We received a call from him, and he asked if he could stay with us. I was skeptical. I had only seen Terry a handful of times in the last twenty years. I didn't know him anymore. I also knew that he was a homeless, forty-year-old man with addictions and mental issues, and that was not a good combination with my family with young children.

I told him he could visit for a few days, and we would decide later if he could move in with us.

Terry behaved while he was visiting, and we had let him stay with us, but we did not drink alcohol or smoke, so it was difficult for him to find any substances to abuse. He had to walk over a mile to the nearest gas station, and this may have proved to be a challenge for him to find alcohol. He enjoyed the serenity of the mountains. He loved to read books and take bike rides. He was always planning and packing for a hiking trip.

He spent many hours in his room sleeping. He would cry for days at a time and even started yelling random things when he was left alone for too long. He tended to mix up his nights with his days and go days without eating. When Reed's older sister Anna moved in with us, she and Terry became good friends, and he had someone he could talk to and watch movies with. He helped her to recover from knee surgery and found himself useful. He started to make an improvement.

I took him several times to visit counselors, but he refused to take medications. He said he felt worse taking them. One time, I received a phone call from a stranger at a park, at a phone booth in Ogden, Utah. He said there is a man here that appears lost, and he had this phone number in his wallet. I went to get Terry. He had a lapse in where he thought he saw our mom and Kristen driving past in a car, and he took off after them on foot. He couldn't understand why they didn't stop. He missed his children terribly and was always planning a way to get back to Farmington, New Mexico, to visit them.

He lived with us for about four years. During that time, he was incarcerated three times for alcohol-related incidents. Every time he would catch a bus to Salt Lake City, he would manage to get himself arrested over some alcohol offense. We lost count of how many times he had been incarcerated over the course of his life. We just picked him up and welcomed him warmly when he was ready to get out. Just like Scott, his alcohol demons were more than he could handle. He did not have control of his life.

On one occasion, Reed and I returned from a vacation. We were gone for ten days and had our other children go to our married children's homes. Terry was home alone for ten days. It proved to be a big mistake.

When we got home, Terry was acting out. He was agitated. He wouldn't look me in the eye when I tried to talk to him at the kitchen counter. I noticed out of the corner of my eye that he grabbed a very sharp letter opener and started running down the stairs to our son, Lucas's room.

"Terry!" I shouted. "Stop!"
Reed heard me yell and came running behind me down to Lucas's room. Reed's sister Anna heard the commotion and came running too.

Terry ran into the bedroom, standing over the bed with rustled up blankets and started stabbing the blankets. Thank God Lucas was not in the bed!

Lucas was sitting across the room in a high-back office chair looking at a computer. He swiveled the chair around and said, "What's up, Terry?"

Lucas then jumped to his feet as he saw Terry raised the letter opener above his head. I was entering the room now and grabbed Terry around the neck with my arm. Lucas grabbed the letter opener and then grabbed Terry's wrists. We struggled for a minute, but Terry knew he was defeated with two of us.

Terry started sobbing. He didn't want to look at us. Lucas gently asked, "What's wrong, Terry?" I was stunned. I couldn't believe what Terry just tried to do. After nearly four years of no problems, he just snapped.

Anna put her arms around Terry and kept telling him, "I love you." Terry cried harder. I wanted to console him too, but the anger from someone trying to hurt one of my children was conflicting within me, and I just needed to stay neutral.

I told Terry this changed everything, and unless he came with me to the emergency room to be self-admitted, he could not stay with us any longer. Anna volunteered to go with us.

We barely made it into the parking lot of the hospital, and Terry opened the door and took off running. He ran between the buildings, and I could no longer see him.

I walked into the emergency room and told them what just happened and asked what I should do. The front desk said they couldn't do anything because he had to be self-admitted. They did say that the security was watching on camera, and they were sure they would go talk to him.

I walked around outside, and I noticed a security guard was talking to him. I started to walk slowly over to him wondering if I should say something. The guard motion for me to come over. He asked me if I wanted to say anything to Terry. In the meantime, he had called on his radio for backup.

I told Terry that I couldn't take him home. He had to get help in order to stay with us. Within a minute, the Ogden Police Department had a car pulled up to us and asked what was going on. I explained what Terry needed to do, and the officer told me it was okay to leave now, that he would take care of Terry.

A few hours later, the psychiatric department of the University of Utah Hospital called to let me know that soon after I left, Terry resisted the officer, and so he was arrested. The officer brought Terry to the hospital, and Terry went crazy on them, so they sedated him. The nurse said she would call us back with updates.

Two days later, I got a call that Terry didn't wake up like they expected him to do, so they left him alone in an unguarded room. Somehow, Terry slipped out, and no one knew where he was. She asked if I knew where he was.

I didn't know where he was. I called his children in New Mexico to ask if they had seen him; they said no. I called my mother in Kansas to see if he was there, and she said no. However, she divulged to me that Terry called her while I was on vacation and told her he was hearing voices in his head telling him to kill people. I was shocked Mom did not call me and tell me that as soon as I came back!

The next day, I got a call from Terry. He was in Farmington, New Mexico. I am not sure how he managed to get a ride down there. He was happy to be around his children, but they were not happy to have him around. He had immediately started drinking, and two of his teen sons were upset.

Little Terry was nineteen at the time, working and renting an apartment. He quit school and was working on one of the oil rigs. He and Josh were thrown out of their home by their new stepdad. His brother Josh was seventeen and was living with him. Josh had dropped out of school a year earlier and was struggling emotionally with the contention he faced with his new stepdad and his own father's problems.

In a few days, Terry called me and was crying. His son Josh was in the hospital from an overdose. Terry wanted to know how he could help him. I explained in the kindest way I could to Terry that he was not in a position to help his son. My husband had taught me to be frank with other men, not to sugarcoat things because men can sense when you are not being direct with them. I told Terry he needed to get his own life back in order and get back on social security disability so that he won't be a financial drain on his sons. He promised me he would step back and try to stabilize his own life so he would not disrupt his son's fragile environment.

Terry began drinking heavily when he hung up. His son Little Terry came home from work and found his dad crying and threatening suicide. Little Terry, in frustration, said to his dad, "Dad, you threaten us with that every time you get drunk. Stop it."

His father opened the kitchen drawer, pulled out a small handgun, held it to the back of his head, and said, "You don't think I will do it, do you?"

In a matter of seconds, Terry pulled the trigger, and his body dropped lifeless to the floor. He was lying on the floor in a pool of blood.

"Oh God—no!" Little Terry cried out as he ran to his father's body. He called 9-1-1, but his dad was gone immediately. His father knew exactly where to point the gun—at the base of his skull—to die instantaneously.

Little Terry called me and asked, "When are you coming down to arrange the funeral for my dad?" I forgot for a moment that I was my brother's caregiver and there really wasn't anyone else to be in charge. I left for New Mexico the next morning to put on a funeral for my brother. My last two children were in junior high, and Reed stayed home to take care of them. I was adamant that my children must not be exposed to this culture of suicide. I did not take them to my sister's funeral, and I did not want them at my brother's funeral either.

The funeral was a continuation of how the family dynamics played out. My mom behaved as if she didn't know why life was so hard for Terry, and she felt helpless in dealing with him. She also pitched the manipulation that she probably couldn't go to her own son's funeral because she had no gas money.

I sent her the money. I also knew that meant she wasn't helping to pay for the funeral either. I debated with myself whether I should be blunt with her for the first time and say something like, "Scott, Kristen, and Terry have miserable lives because you didn't protect them when Dad died. Instead, you dragged them through wretched conditions, exposed them to substance abuse, and displayed a lack of judgment in subjecting them to Carson and his alcoholic behaviors that destroyed any security or sanity in all of your lives." Once again, I just kept things to myself.

My brother Jerry showed up with his wife and some of their children and grandchildren. It was nice they supported the family, but they questioned me about not having my husband and children there. I wasn't offended, just reluctant.

I couldn't tell them I didn't think it was right to expose my children to this or it would insult them for bringing their children and grandchildren. I made up my mind years ago not to take my children to suicide funerals or expose them to any tragic events stemming from the dysfunction of my side of the family. I also did not want my children to absorb unnecessary pain and empathy on my behalf as children. I would tell them later as adults. Jerry's children were adults, and it wouldn't have the same effect.

The funeral service was actually one of the stronger spiritual moments in my life. I could feel a sense of peace resting on me. I had a fuller perspective now on suicide. I had been through this a few times now.

I knew that Terry was hurting and needed a compassionate release from this world. I watched him over the years literally go mentally crazy because he could not handle the depression and agony. I knew he was being cared for and was relieved of his earthly burdens that became too great to bear. I knew that God loved him and did not banish him to hell. I knew he was welcomed by our loved ones upon crossing over. I knew he was finally experiencing joy.

There are a lot of opinions from many religious backgrounds as to suicide and the judgment of it. Most people make comments that are ugly and mean about suicide when often they have never experienced losing a loved one to suicide. It is usually said to protect others from considering suicide themselves or it is a knee-jerk reaction to not understanding the depths of despair someone else could possibly go through.

When I had the dream where my father was standing in the field, I knew then that people who commit suicide are not banished to hell. I am sure he is doing a lot of repenting and going through some corrective measures and possibly giving up some greater heavenly conditions, but he would not have been allowed to visit me in my dream if he was in hell.

I contemplated that if there was a judgment day as described in the Bible, it says that judgment day is after the millennium (a period of a thousand years after the end times). I knew my father and my brother were not judged the day they died because judgment day is still yet to come.

Another comfort I found was that the word *suicide* does not exist in the Bible. The interpretation of what suicide is comes from well-meaning clergy, but ultimately it is not detailed in the scriptures. It is not for us to judge another human over it. I had felt deep in my heart that God knew some of his children would not be able to sustain the burdens of mortality. Only he could judge them on a case-by-case basis. Only he could know that person's heart and that person's despair.

It is hard for some people to imagine the very act of suicide as being anything but selfish. I went to a holiday dinner with my husband, and a woman at the table, not knowing anything about me, tried to start a conversation by stating her day had been ruined.

Using her disgusted voice, she ranted on that one of her children's friends just lost her father to suicide. She carried on, "How could he be so selfish. This is Christmas after all! I don't know how anyone could do that to their family. He is a real pig."

Needless to say, I saddened that her perception was so limited and I had to refrain from getting upset, but I used my patient voice and assured her, "This father would not have done that if he were in his right mind and wasn't dealing with some very real internal pain. We cannot judge what his motives were." I then shared that I had lost a father, brother, and sister to suicide. The subject was dropped, and we got on with the dinner.

In reality, the pain and struggle inside someone who is contemplating suicide is so awful that a person becomes consumed with despair and pain; they become irrational because they are experiencing too much pain at one time. That agony doesn't go away. They cannot find relief.

If there is anything I could do in this life to make the world a better place, it would be to comfort others who have experienced someone committing suicide in the family. When the devil visits, we can slam the door shut and chase him off our porch. It doesn't have to be a blot in the family history, or be kept a secret. Suicide doesn't have to stop those left behind from going on to live an incredible life, although it feels like life will never be normal again. We can take that trauma and turn it into something meaningful.

We can allow ourselves to be filled with compassion. We can help others navigate through the despair we ourselves once experienced. We can remove suicide as an option with others by talking about it. We can comfort others who experience the same tragedy and save them years of useless pain.

Many times suicide becomes environmental because once people are exposed to a suicide, they themselves become consumed with trying to understand it. It is so traumatic for those left behind, and it is hard to describe how the hole in your heart never closes. Mourning a loved one who has taken their own life is not the same as when someone dies a normal death. For most, every time we despair, depressed, or overwhelmed, our thoughts consider suicide as an option because it is now a part of who we are.

Survivors spend hours contemplating the final hours of a loved one and what they must have gone through. We comb over all the details wondering if we could have gone through the act ourselves, if we could have said something to change the outcome, helped the victim early on, or even noticed if they were in this state of mind.

We worry about the afterlife and all the things we have been taught or read about. We mourn for them again and again, over and over decades later. We love the person who died so much it is hard to see how God could cut them off, punish them, or not have compassion for them.

God does love them. I know that as sure as I know the sun will shine tomorrow. I have that peace and confirmation that can only come from him. He is greater than we are. We are his creation, and he knew there would be many who could not endure all that earth life might press upon us.

In order for me to move forward, I had to let it go and trust that God knows what is best for all of us and that he is merciful; otherwise, I would be angry and feel injustice.

Until I refused to allow any thoughts of a God who was anything but merciful, just and full of love, I could not stop worrying and crying for those who have passed on. Once I developed faith in God's fairness, I could finally crawl out of that hole of pain and despair.

I struggled with the outcomes of my siblings' lives wondering if it would have been better if none of us were ever born. After much pondering, I realized that we were born to experience good and evil. If our lives were comfortable and painless, we should have just stayed in heaven where there is no evil. It was having experiences away from God's presence that would help us to progress and grow. No matter how tragic or terrifying the experience was, we would, as Eve said in the garden, "have our eyes opened, knowing good from evil."

I truly believe that no struggle or pain we suffer is ever wasted. All that we suffer builds up our character and changes us. We learn from our difficulties. My siblings' lives had meaning despite their failures.

I will always love my siblings no matter what they have done. I will always see them as the children I nurtured and cared for when they were young. I still have survivor's guilt. I feel guilty that I am the one who got away and they got stuck. I feel guilty that I could not rescue them. I feel guilty that I went on to live a life of love and renewal and they never came close. I am not surprised the younger ones died before me. They didn't stand a chance being the younger siblings left in the care of my mother through a tragedy.

A Tender Farewell

My mother called me a few months after Terry's death. She wanted me to come visit her while she was spending time in Texas on one of Carson's construction jobs. I had only seen her one other time while she lived in Kansas, and that was for Kristen's funeral.

"Hey, do you think you could come visit me while I am in Texas this summer? Will that be easier for you to fly into? I need to talk to you. I feel like I am being prepared to die," she said over the phone.

I said, "Of course, I would. Give me the dates."
She was in Corpus Christi, Texas, staying in a fifth-wheel trailer at an RV park. Carson was on a crew to install large windmills that generated electricity. My mom was a heavy smoker, so most of the day we spent outside in the heavy humidity under the awning in lawn chairs so she could smoke a cigarette.

My first night there, we went to a Chinese restaurant.The conversation was pleasant, and we made jokes about the shrimp running off our plates with their tiny legs as we used our tiny voices to scream, "Help me, help me." Mom and I had worked out the chemistry between us that was palatable to us both. We could be friends. I would tolerate Carson and recognize that he was her choice. I would be civil and leave it up to God to judge him. She would stop playing the role of victim and stop manipulating me into her helping her financially or believing in her half-truths about the past.

The first thing I noticed was that Carson turned a tool chest that stretched across the back of his truck into an ice chest to hold several cans of beer. He always had a beer in his hand. It was the first thing he drank in the morning, with lunch, for a snack, and with dinner. It was his "water."

Carson was what we called a big talker. He was forward, friendly, and could come up with the biggest stories. He called all women "darling." He, too, was a heavy smoker. The smell of smoke immediately took me back to my childhood where the smell was in my hair, clothes, and house. I was so glad I escaped that culture. I tolerated Carson for my mother's sake. I refused to be combative or disrespectful, but I could never embrace him as a stepfather, and he knew it.

Carson would be gone during the day, and Mom and I could talk freely. She shared with me that she was having heart problems, and no doctor was willing to operate on an aneurism she had. She felt like she was being prepared to die.

We talked about what it would be like to cross over, to see loved ones like Grandma, Dad, Kristen, Mechelle, and Terry. We talked about what she wanted for a funeral. She didn't want her funeral at a church. She wanted to be cremated and buried next to her sister Carolyn in Tescott, Kansas.

It may seem creepy to some people to talk about funeral arrangements and the feeling that you are going to die soon, but this conversation had a sweet, peaceful feeling to it.

Then, she wanted to apologize to me for any pain she may have caused me in my life. I was stunned. All I could think was, *Oh my God, why is she doing that?*

I had spent years propping myself up not to hate her and to accept her the way she was. I felt like a fish being gutted right now.

"No, Mom, you don't have to say anything. I think we are okay," I said.

All the while, I wanted the subject to change. I didn't want to go there. I wasn't sure if I had forgiven her, but I didn't want to be confronted with it in front of her. After all, if I became angry, then she would win. That's what I held on to for thirty years! I was going to win this battle. I was going to take the higher road, and asking my forgiveness somehow undermined all that.

It never crossed my mind that Mom would ever ask for my forgiveness, so I never thought it through or prepared myself should that ever happen.

The trip was short, it was humid and hot, we had a pedicure together, and I found a fabulous salsa recipe. Carson got a case of gout in his arm and had to be admitted into the emergency room the day I had to leave. Mom was distracted and needed to attend to him. I quietly slipped out to go back to the airport. No emotional good-byes, just a quick hug and a promise to call more often.

I flew home anxious to get back to Reed and the children. That was where my connection to love really was. That was where I was safe and could grow in my soul. I loved my mom, but I just didn't know how to love her.

Two months later, the phone call came. Carson was on the other end, sounding hysterical. "She's gone," he said.

I said, "What do you mean, she's gone?" My first thought was she left him.

"She's gone. She died. She fell down the stairs on the trailer, turned to grab the handrail, and hit her head on the concrete slab at the bottom. She got a hematoma on the back of her head, and she died shortly after I got her to the hospital. She's gone." He stopped talking. He didn't really want to talk anymore.

"Call me back when you have made arrangements for the funeral," I said.

I hung up and buried my face into Reed's chest. I cried a little.

Then, there it was, all that anger I was never going to show toward her all those years came to the surface. I was shocked. I didn't even know it existed.

It was like a volcano erupting. It just kept coming. I couldn't sleep, I couldn't focus, and I couldn't put it away. The angry emotions just kept coming. I was no longer in control of my own emotions.

I was feeling some sort of guilt that my mother just died, and I wasn't sad; I was angry at her. Worse than that, I didn't want to go to her funeral. I was done. My thoughts were scattered. *Is this whole nightmare over, or is it not?*

Once again, my heart turned to those who would need me to get through this. There were nieces and nephews planning to be at the funeral. Jerry and Tess were going to be there. Carson tipped off Scott that the FBI was looking for him and were suspicious that he might attend the funeral, so Scott skipped going. Maybe I should put aside my own anger and be a comfort to others.

That's what I would do, I just kept telling myself. I'll take my married daughter, Danielle, with me. She met my mother once when she was a child and seemed to have a connection with her. That will give me someone to talk to and focus my attention on if I find myself going down that vortex of irrational anger and resentment.

I had answers for a lot of things in life. I had fought a good fight so many times and came out the victor, yet I had no answers now. I just wanted this all to be over so I could shut that door.

I went to her funeral; I didn't shed a tear. In fact, I became angrier every time someone came up to me and hugged me. Each well-meaning person would say something like, "I just loved your mother," "She was my best friend," "She would do anything for me," "She would teach me this," "She nursed me back to health," or "She knew how to cheer me up."

Oh, how my heart ached. How I would have loved for my mother to do any of those things for me or with me just one time.

There was a graveside memorial just as she requested. There was no burial as her ashes were not ready yet. Her friend Sue down the street invited everyone over for a luncheon in her yard after.

It would take a few years before the anger stopped surfacing daily. For the first time in my life, I couldn't contain feelings by my own will. I needed help. I had realized that burying feelings only causes them to emerge later. Those feelings never die until you resolve them. I had to ask for divine intervention. I struggled with guilt that I was even feeling angry. If I truly believed in God, I wouldn't have those feelings.

I also took this time to do some introspection about my own mothering skills. Was I too detached at times? Could I have been better at mothering my children? Did I support them in their activities and find ways to encourage and praise them? Did I tell them that I loved them often? I realized how the smallest of words and comments would stick with children throughout their lives.

I would have short periods of time when I thought I was free from my feelings toward my mother, but any conversation or pondering about the family always led me right back to anger and complete despair that I could not move on from this in my life. I lived thirty years of showing empathy and compassion, why could I not have those feelings again?

The final resting moment came when I had a dream, and my mother came to visit me. She was beautiful. She looked about the age of thirty something. Her hair was very dark and in a short haircut. She had a sapphire-blue dress on and a darling figure. She was with an escort named Philip. I didn't know who he was, but I knew he was "teaching" her. I just "knew" his name in my mind as they approached.

Her eyes were as blue as her dress, and they were lit up like there was fire inside them. She looked at me as she walked toward me and kindly said, "I don't have to be your mother, you know." She smiled and then I woke up.

I felt a small amount of shame because I was still harboring anger toward her after her death, yet I knew why she was telling me this. She knew I was still struggling and couldn't really move on wholly until I released her.

It was not hard to see that forgiveness was not for the offender, but for the person who had been wronged. I still had not forgiven her fully up to that point. It was easier to hang on to a few pebbles of pain to self-soothe with. I could be the victim again and again when I needed to elicit sympathy and comforting from others. Not anymore. I recognized the power in her message to me. By releasing her, I could be whole again.

Forgiveness meant I could find peace, hope, gratitude, and joy. It also meant that I could start to recognize that suppressing these feelings only led to further health problems for me. It was not coincidental that I was diagnosed with an autoimmune disease shortly after she died.

The pain in my spine, hips, and neck had been excruciating. The more emotional pain I absorbed from past traumatic events, the more pain cycles I would endure. Although I still have the disease, I have learned how to manage the pain, and removing those unhealthy mental issues from my past has made a great improvement to my health.

Once I embraced that forgiveness is a decision to let go of resentment and anger, it also meant I didn't have to forget what it was that hurt me, but by forgiving it would lessen its grip on me and help me to focus on other positive parts of my life.

I would have to tell myself, *If you're unforgiving, you repeatedly bring anger and bitterness into every relationship. You become depressed. You feel that your life lacks meaning or purpose. You lose connectedness with others.*

Forgiveness didn't mean that I deny the other person's responsibility for hurting me, and it didn't minimize or justify the wrong. I can forgive the person without excusing the act. Forgiveness brings a kind of peace that helps me go on with life.

I started to study the Atonement of Jesus Christ even more. I soon discovered that his sacrifice on the cross was more than just for repentance of sins, it was also for all the wrongs ever done. It was for healing and restoring of those things that we as humans do not have the power to do. I realized that no matter how strong I had been to this point, no matter how hard I tried to do all of this on my own, some things require more than prayer. Some things require fasting. All things require petitioning the Lord for his power to heal as he will not intervene with our agency.

When I read this, it made perfect sense to me. It helped me to let go. I didn't need to worry about fairness or justice; God would take care of that. I just needed to get on with my life, make happy memories, and prepare my children for an awesome life.

A year after my mother's death, things did not end well for Little Terry either. I begged him to get some help for witnessing his father's suicide. He insisted he was going to be fine. He said he didn't blame himself for what for what his father did. He joined the marines the next month and was stationed in Japan later that year. He even married his sweetheart, Emilee.

I got a call from his grandfather, Pat, that Little Terry took his life on his lunch hour. He hung himself in the closet with his belt. We can only assume he was haunted by his father's death. One night when drinking with some buddies, he had a breakdown and started crying out. He said, "I don't deserve to live. Just shoot me, let me die!"

Of course, that prompted the military to put him on suicide watch. The day he got off the suicide watch, he took his life.

One of the hardest things I have ever had to reconcile was the image of a twenty-one-year-old marine lying in a casket at Christmastime because he was unable to find the strength to push away the generations of tragedy and sickness. Even in the arms of a loving new wife and the isolation of a new place on the other side of the world, he didn't stand a chance.

I searched the Internet for a book to send to his widow and to his mother. I ended up sending several books in hopes that something would resonate with them or bring them comfort. Something that stuck out in my mind and brought some relief to me in one of the books, *Why People Die by Suicide* by Thomas Joiner, was a theory that there are three types of people.

One type was a group of people who could never commit suicide. These people never think about it, nor is it an option for them to solve their life's problems. These same people have a difficult time understanding how anyone else could commit suicide. These are the people who get angry and upset when they hear that someone has committed suicide and exhibit no understanding or empathy. My husband would fit in this category, and the lady who was seated at my holiday dinner table would also be in this category.

The second type of person is one who thinks about suicide, entertains the thoughts of suicide, been exposed to suicide, and is not afraid to talk about it. This person, however, lacks the will to commit suicide. This person has a strong sense of the destruction that would follow and cannot bring themselves to do it. I was relieved to see myself fit this category. I hate that suicide is always in the shadows of my thoughts. It is in me because of my exposure to it, I vowed years ago to recognize its destruction and not succumb to the enticing thoughts and feelings of relief.

Then there is the third type of person who has the will. This person can think about suicide once or many times, they have a plan, and they have no problem acting on it. This was my brother Terry, his son Little Terry, my father, and probably my sister.

These categories have helped me to hone in on each of my children and evaluate if any one might be at risk. It would help me take extra precautions if I detect any signs. I am at peace for now.

I do worry about my brother Scott. Scott's alcohol addictions have kept him incarcerated most of his adult life. He tries really hard to be a good citizen when he gets out, but the temptation for alcohol is too strong. It is like being in a prison without fences for him. His life is dictated by the things he cannot control.

Scott has called me several times and broke down crying. He misses the loved ones that have now passed away. He misses his kids who are now absent in his life. There is no one to support and care for him. I still worry about him every time he gets out. I worry that one day, he, too, will give up the fight. I have asked him straight up if he ever considers suicide. He just looked at me like I was crazy and shook his head no. I needed to know. Only time will tell, but now I am a little more at peace.

THE PILLARS IN MY LIFE

There was one other dream that I had twice as a young woman around the age of twelve. I didn't fully understand its significance until much later in my life. It was vivid like the others. I'm not sure why I had it twice except that maybe I needed to remember it.

In my dream, I was standing on a large set of concrete steps with large white pillars on each side of me. I was standing there with a man next to me. I couldn't see my husband's face; I just knew that was who it was. We were both dressed in white clothing, which I felt was symbolic of righteousness and fidelity.

We were greeting others who would come up the steps and shake their hands. We would hand them things, although I don't recall specifically the details of those "things," but I knew it was what they needed, and it was helping them.

I loved this dream because I felt romantic love. I felt commitment from another person. I felt that I was important because I was serving others rather than being dependent on others. It was like a "princess story" that little girls daydream about. Little did I know at the time, the Lord was placing a marker in my life.

When I turned forty, we were having a home built. It was a miraculous move because for the first time, we could control our financial future and could move anywhere we wanted, as we had a home business. We were being blessed financially from a business I started to put our children through college. We would also be able to continue helping others by having an apartment built in the basement of our new home.

We had moved to a tucked-away community to live in peace away from the troubles of city life behind the Wasatch Mountains in Utah. These mountains are among the most serene views on earth.

One day I was zooming up the long, cemented driveway in my car in an upward motion, and I looked up briefly just in time to catch the large, cemented front porch having the white pillars installed. There it was, my dream flashing in my mind. The layout was identical to the dream. I felt so humble. I had to stop the car.

Tears swelled up in my eyes, and my heart was feeling warm. I recognized immediately that it was a message of love from a God who knew how my life would end up when I was but a young girl and that I would need these dreams later as a confirmation that God was with me all along.

In today's society, it is all the rage to be an intellectual and to shun religion as archaic and unnecessary. I am here to tell you nothing could be farther from the truth. People are physical and spiritual matter. The more you develop faith, the more you find God. Whether it is in dreams, personal revelation, books you read, or just the warm feelings in your heart, once you experience his touch and your mind is open by his Spirit, you cannot deny that God exists. He will work miracles in your life and give you the advantage you need as you progress through this channel of learning known as earth life.

God usually answers prayers through other people. He blesses those whom he can trust with resources to help others. We are to abide in faith, hope, and charity; but charity is the greatest of them all.

I hesitate to talk about the numerous acts of charity our family has been involved in because it is personal and somewhat sacred. However, there are some stories that needed to be shared because of the outcome of some of the stories shared in this book.

We have been fortunate to have Terry's two remaining children, Joshua and Isis, live with us. Joshua has graduated now from a computer tech school and is working at an aviation company as a computer tech.

We have had the blessing of helping Kristen's children—David, Timothy and Michael—reunite after being separated from each other for seventeen years. We have been able to be of help in other ways in their lives, hiring them for projects and having them take a ski vacation at our home with us. Timothy is living with us now.

The same goes for Scott's children. We have been able to be a support to Claudette and Shari when they have needed help or encouragement. I did not have the privilege of watching any of these nieces and nephews grow up or spend time with them in their youth, but I can say I have the same pride and love for them as if I had known them my whole life.

We have been able to help my brother Scott with housing, transportation, and other personal resources when he was released on parole from prison. It is nearly impossible for parolees to assimilate back into society without some kind of support and resources. We have and will be there again and again. Although he was incarcerated again this year, we will write him and encourage him like we always have.

If you were to ask me *how did I overcome all of this*, I would tell you it took four things: 1. Get out of your toxic environment. Move out, find others willing to take you in, keep distance between you and those who are emotional vampires. 2. Get an education. It is nearly impossible to become self-sufficient without an education. Pay the price. Get it done. 3. Develop a relationship with God. You cannot expect miracles if you lack the faith in God to receive them. 4. Rebuild your life with your own definition of success. For me, there is no higher calling, than that of motherhood. All the other successes came from having my family life in order.

The foundation in my life is having a strong family bond with my spouse and children. That is where I can create a new world of safety, love, and peace. I get to be the architect of the traditions, happiness, and memories. You've heard the expression "Childhood is what you spend your adulthood getting over." Well, I say, "Adulthood is where you get to redo your childhood!" You can replace those bad memories with good ones.

About fifteen years ago, I learned just how deep God's love is for all his children. My life would come full circle as I had an experience that would shock me to my core.

It was April 1, 1999. It was spring break for the kids, it was Easter for the kids, it was also two weeks before the IRS tax deadline, and that meant that Reed was not available for us to go somewhere, as he was a tax preparer in addition to his regular job. The weather in California was warm, and the trees were in full bloom. The sound of a mini vacation was calling me.

I loaded up all seven of the kids in the van and told Reed I was taking them to Utah to visit his mother. The children loved to go to Grandma's, and for the most part, they loved road trips. It was only twelve hours, I could drive through the night while the children were sleeping, and I was feeling adventurous.

We had to pass over High Sierra Mountains just before Reno, and then it is basically desert until you get to Salt Lake City. So it was surprising that when I got to the top of the summit, traffic was being stopped while the highway patrol assessed whether the cars can go through without chains. I was just about to turn around and return to Sacramento when they opened the road as clear. I was relieved to go on. I turned the heater on, but for some reason, it wasn't working. I figured I wouldn't need it once I got to the desert portion of the trip.

After leaving Reno, the snowstorm got worse. The roads were covered with snow, and all I could do was follow the truckers in hopes of seeing the tracks they left in the snow. I could only follow close enough to keep the snow from being sprayed all over my wind shield and blinding me. I was shocked it was snowing this hard!

I had no clue there would be a storm this late in the year. I just kept plugging along, hoping to find a small town with a hotel.

Eventually, I pulled over and got a room. We were freezing with the snow coming down so heavy. I had to put the air conditioner on to stop the windows from fogging up, and that made it so we all had to wrap blankets around us to survive the cold.

I decided to wake the kids up early and get on the road because the storm wasn't stopping, and I didn't want to be snowed in! I pulled into Wendover, a small town in Nevada on the Utah border, for breakfast at around six in the morning. It was only two more hours from there to Reed's mother's house.

The kids piled out of the van and waited patiently at the table, like they were instructed. In fact, we had strict rules for public places when we were all together like this. Each kid was assigned a buddy, and they were responsible for the other child, making sure they had what they needed. All I needed to do was to order food and serve them. Everything went as planned. A woman even came up to me and complimented me on how great my kids were since I had so many and was alone.

I saw the storm starting again and told the kids to hurry up and get in the van so we could outrun it. Just then, Lucas asked me what he should do. He said Hannah, his buddy, who was about six years old, was in the bathroom, but he couldn't go get her because he was a boy. I handed him my eighteen-month-old and told him to go buckle the baby in and I would take care of Hannah.

I decided to tuck the kids in their blankets, who returned to sleep immediately, and closed the van door to keep the snow out while I was waiting for Hannah. Then, without another thought, I jumped in the driver seat and started driving down the road.

About ten minutes out of town, I got this very strong feeling that someone is missing. I laughed to myself and said, "I'm not falling for that feeling anymore. I have all the kids I am supposed to have. No more babies for me."

I turned the radio on low, and about thirty minutes later, I got the same strong feeling that someone is missing. I immediately blocked the thought with a memory of our friends who also had a large family and they accidentally left one of their children at a Taco Bell in another state! *That wouldn't happen to us, we have a buddy system.*

Just as I was entering the Salt Lake Valley, we were about ten minutes from where Grandma lived, Lucas sat up and said, "Mom, where's Hannah?"

"Oh my God!" I screamed. At that very moment, I realized what I had done. I started to go into a zone as if I was going to pass out. I was light-headed, things were spinning, and it was starting to go dark. I kept calling to myself, *Don't pass out, you will crash!*

Then I had this great urge to throw up. I had to repeat to myself again, *Don't do it, you will crash. Take the kids to Grandma's so they can get out of the cold van and go back for her.*

I immediately asked my son to say a prayer aloud for Hannah. By now, all the kids were awake, and we were going through the instructions for when we get to Grandma's in a few minutes. Each child took a turn praying for Hannah. Finally, we reached Grandma's trailer. I ran out of the van and started banging on her locked door. She wasn't awake yet. She was expecting us later that day. She came to the door with a sour look on her face. She thought I was being rude banging so hard. Just then, I heard the phone ringing.

I asked her, "Please ask whoever is calling to hang up, I have an emergency."

"You answer the phone and tell them to hang up!" she snapped back at me.

"Hello?" I asked while holding the phone to my ear.

"Is this the McDermott's?" asked the male voice on the other end.

"Yes, this is the McDermott's," I answered but was just about to ask them to hang up when the caller interrupted.

"This is Officer Smith. I have your daughter Hannah," he said.

I burst into a loud cry and fell on the floor. I was so happy but so overwhelmed at the same time.

"Take a minute, Hannah is okay," he said. There was about ten seconds of silence before I could utter a word.

"How did you find us?" I asked through the tears.

"Hannah told us she was visiting Grandma McDermott in Utah. So we went through the phone book and started calling all the McDermotts in the Salt Lake Valley," he said.

"You just happened to reach the right McDermott in the phone book when I walked in the door ready to call the police myself," I said as I still lay on the floor curled up trying to clear up my sobbing. My kids just stood around waiting for the news that Hannah was found.

"How did you find her?" I asked.

"There was a woman who watched you in the restaurant and then watched you load up your children. Within minutes, she saw your daughter come out of the bathroom, walk outside, and put her head down when she saw you driving off. She immediately pulled Hannah to her table and waited about thirty minutes for you to come back. When you didn't, she flagged down a patrol officer who was cutting through the parking lot. She told us you were travelling with multiple children, and you were alone. She said it was an easy mistake." He spoke calmly.

"I am so sorry, this should have never happened," I said.

"There is a big storm still going on. You should wait a few hours before coming back. Please be careful driving," he said.

I couldn't wait a few hours. All I knew was Hannah was safe, but she was not with me. I just needed to get back to her. I asked Lucas to ride back with me. I figured they wouldn't arrest me if I had another child with me. We drove back breaking the speed limit. I wrapped towels around my feet to keep them from freezing as the air conditioner had to be on. The storm was worse than when we came through it an hour ago.

Lucas and I walked into the police station. There was no one at the front desk, but there were several offices surrounding the desk. Soon an officer walked in, and I immediately said, "I'm Hannah's mom."

His face lit up and said, "Oh hi, I'll be back."

Another officer came out of his office, then another, then another. I'm sure when they heard who I was, and they wanted to see what kind of mother would leave her child at a restaurant for over two hours before realizing she was missing! Just then, Hannah came out of the conference room with a McDonald's bag. She started to run toward me, and I went down on my knees to hug her.

"Why did you leave me?" she said with a disappointing tone.

"Honey, Mommy didn't leave you on purpose. I just forgot you were in the bathroom. Please forgive me." I hugged her tight.

"Mommy, these are my friends," she said as she pointed to the officers.

"I know, the police are nice. Honey, say good-bye, we need to go now."

"No, Mommy, I want to finish the movie."

"No, we have to go now, say good-bye."

With tears rolling down my cheeks, I thanked the officers and scuttled Hannah and Lucas out of there before they changed their mind about me.

We immediately went to an automotive repair shop a block away and had an eleven-dollar heat thermometer replaced. We drove back in comfort.

I had two hours to think on my drive back, cry all over again, and review all the emotions I went through. I reviewed all the bad things that could have happened. In today's world, someone could have harmed her, and I could have never seen Hannah again. I would have never forgiven myself.

What came to me next was the assurance that in my darkest moment of gut-wrenching despair that with all the love I felt for my child, God loved each of us just the same and with his divinity, even more. I thought of my family members who had passed on and how much God must love them, and just as I was willing to risk my life through a snowstorm to get Hannah back, God was willing to give his son to bring us all back to him.

The McDermotts—2011

For additional photos, comments, or purchases
visit our photo gallery at:
www.whenthedevilvisits.com

CPSIA information can be obtained
at www.ICGtesting.com
Printed in the USA
LVOW04s1132141215
466570LV00030B/1765/P